The Export Adventurer

This third edition.

First published in Great Britain in 2026

Copyright © Gerald Bratley 2019, 2022, 2026

Gerry Bratley has asserted his moral right to be identified as the Author of this Work in accordance with the Copyright Designs and Patents Act 1988.

All rights reserved. No part of this book may be reproduced or utilised in any form or by any means, electronic or mechanical, including photocopying, recording or by any information storage and retrieval system, without permission in writing from Gerald Bratley

A catalogue record for this book is available from the British Library.

ISBN 9798370867729

The Export Adventurer

I dedicate this book to the memory of
the best boss and people manager
I ever encountered.
My good friend
George Bell

The Export Adventurer

Table of Contents

Introduction 1
Chapter 1 — Starting Work 4
Chapter 2 — The 'Copper Works' (Yorkshire Imperial Metals Limited) 9
    Export Department 9
    The information system 11
    Work on your feet 12
    Calculations 12
    Correspondence 14
    The world arrives on your desk 15
    Metrication and the home market surprise 16
    A sideways "promotion" 17
    The annealed tubes letter 17
    Social life and the mill's sense of humour 18
    Looking back 21
Chapter 3 — Marriage and Serious Money 23
    Square onions and eggs 24
    Bratley Newton Associates 25
Chapter 4 — BNA-Gowanbury Limited 27
    Leaving the Copper Works 29
    Big projects and bigger trust 29
    Turning specifications to advantage 31
    Logistics at scale 31

Success, missteps and consequences	32
Bahrain and beyond	33
Chapter 5 — Italrad	**35**
Forming Italrad	35
European road trips	36
Fuel, favours and funerals	37
Alloy wheels and Italian strikes	38
Success — and saturation	39
Chapter 6 — Marley Extrusions	**40**
The merry-go-round	43
Chapter 7 — Bartol Plastics	**46**
Putting systems in place	47
New markets, new thinking	49
Ireland and Europe	50
How to find markets	50
Chapter 8 — First Choice — The Preparation	**52**
Chapter 9 — Baghdad Fair	**56**
Chapter 10 — The Baghdad Sewerage Board	**62**
Chapter 11 — The Iraq Market	**69**
Watching the company from afar	72
Alan Nelson: time, nerves, and "Engineer Akmed"	72
Breakfast, logistics, and tea in a coffee cup	73
"Cook, he has no watch"	74
George in Baghdad	75

The Export Adventurer

The Dar es Salaam 76
The seminar, the projector, and the embassy dash.........77
The Sheriff 78
The best plastics man I ever met 79
Beige dust and cornflake engineering...............................82
The wedding and the pressing problem............................82
Shoes, sun, and dignity...84
Smelling the potential..86
Flies, ice, and other Baghdad realities...............................86
"Why do you want to buy a parachute?" 87
    Teaching Cast Iron Men to Trust Plastic 88
    Last Trip to Iraq 90
Chapter 12 — INDIA...96
Chapter 13 — SRI LANKA 101
Chapter 14 — THE CARIBBEAN 105
Chapter 15 — JORDAN 111
Chapter 16 — EGYPT 116
Chapter 17 — LEBANON 121
Chapter 18 — MALAYSIA 125
    The Sng family and the launch plan............................126
    Family life, and the cost of distance.............................127
    Settling in: visas, phones, and early "email" 128
    BAS, TEKSI, and "DADA MEANS DEATH" 130

George in Malaysia: peanuts, morphine, and a windsurfer 130

Building the business: people first, then pipe 131

Life in KL: fast, easy, cheap… and lost spectacles 132

Restaurants, Louis XIII, and tiger prawns 133

Heat, rain, durian, and expat life 134

Doncaster problems, "Ken", and losing face 135

"DADA MEANS DEATH" strikes again: customs and a container 136

The move to Seoul 136

Chapter 19 — WEST AFRICA 138

Nigeria 138

Ghana 143

Togo 144

Côte d'Ivoire 144

The Gambia 145

Sierra Leone 146

Liberia 147

Chapter 20 — Central African Republic 148

Chapter 21 — CONTINENTAL EUROPE 150

CYPRUS 161

MALTA 162

Chapter 22 — IRELAND 164

Chapter 23 — AUSTRALIA 168

Chapter 24 — NEW ZEALAND 173
Chapter 25 — JAPAN 177
Chapter 26 — UNITED STATES 181
Chapter 27 — HONG KONG 185
Chapter 28 — TAIWAN 194
Chapter 29 — THAILAND 198
Chapter 30 — SOUTH KOREA 201
Chapter 31 — ALEXY/ARONSTEAD (final grammar scan) 225
Chapter 32 — ALLIED DUNBAR (final edited version) 227
Chapter 33 — BARNSLEY CHAMBER OF COMMERCE .232
Chapter 34 — DEPARTMENT OF TRADE AND INDUSTRY 241
   Export Promoter — the role 241
   Inward missions, seminars and Korea-focused work 244
   The 1994 UK trade mission to Korea 247
   What it all gave me 249
Chapter 35 — NORTH KOREA 251
   Pyongyang 253
   Five days under escort 255
   Leaving North Korea 257
Chapter 36 — KOREA CONNECTIONS 258
   Formation of Korea Connections 258
   Overview 259

The Export Adventurer

 Cultural Requirements 259
 Dominique Bratley (Cho Hye Young) 260
 Services Offered 261
 Globalisation and Opportunity 261
 Case Studies and Successes 262
 Closing Reflections 264
Chapter 37 — Retirement 265
 The Export Development Service 265
Conclusion 266
APPENDICES .... A
 Appendix I – Airlines Used .... A
 Appendix II – Countries Visited on Business (add 20 more where I have vacated) .... D
 Appendix III – Aircraft Types Flown .... G

The Export Adventurer

Introduction

This book traces a potted history of my working life from 1967 to the present day. It focuses on what was unusual, occasionally hilarious, and sometimes dangerous — the things that never found their way into visit reports or official records. Looking back now, I feel a mixture of pride in what I achieved and gratitude for the privilege of having been allowed to do it, tempered by a quiet regret for opportunities missed and paths not taken.

Over the years, I visited fifty-two countries on business. Some — South Korea, Malaysia, and Hong Kong — I travelled to more than sixty times. Others, including Australia, Taiwan, Jordan, Iraq, and most of Europe, I visited a dozen times or more. That amount of travel, however, does not come without compromise, particularly at home.

I have been both employed and self-employed, in the private and public sectors. I have worked with imports and exports, in manufacturing, finance, and business support, and wherever possible I passed on whatever expertise and experience I had gained. I have seen international trade from almost every conceivable angle.

The Export Adventurer

If there is such a thing as a qualification for this kind of work, it would include being an extrovert, possessing a well-developed sense of humour, and being resilient. Things rarely go to plan.

I have survived several near misses — enough that, but for good fortune, I might not be here today.

On one winter's day, flying from Leeds Bradford to Schiphol on an Air UK Fokker F27 Friendship, the aircraft began to vibrate violently halfway across the North Sea. Without warning, it plunged from cruising height to skim just above the icy water. The vibrations were so severe that I was convinced we were about to ditch. I located my lifejacket under the seat and waited. After what felt like an eternity, the vibrations slowly diminished, the engines began to run smoothly again, and we climbed back to cruising altitude. The pilot later explained that ice had formed on the propellers and that he had dived into warmer air to clear it.

When I first travelled to India with the Huddersfield Chamber of Commerce, I flew on Air India flight 182 from London to Delhi, part of the Toronto–Montreal–London–Delhi route. Just weeks later, on 23 June 1985, that same Boeing 747-237B — registration VT-EFO, *Emperor Kanishka* — disintegrated mid-air at 31,000 feet following a bomb explosion planted by Canadian Sikh terrorists. It crashed into the Atlantic Ocean off the southwest tip of Ireland, killing all 329 people on board.

I have been on two aircraft that aborted landings, both at Leeds Bradford — once due to fog, once because of crosswinds — and was diverted on both occasions. The latter was on a Short 360, a square-looking aircraft with wings mounted above the fuselage and engines suspended just outside the passenger cabin. Inside, it felt like flying a box kite in a gale.

The Export Adventurer

In February 1987, I returned from Zeebrugge to Dover on the Townsend Thoresen ferry *MS Herald of Free Enterprise*. Three weeks later, on the night of 6 March, the vessel capsized moments after leaving the Belgian port, killing 193 passengers and crew.

Later that same year, I passed through King's Cross station on my way to Heathrow on the morning of 18 November. That evening, a fire broke out beneath a wooden escalator serving the Piccadilly Line. At 19:45 it erupted into a flashover in the underground ticket hall, killing thirty-one people and injuring one hundred.

I have flown through war zones escorted by fighters, and on my first visit to Baghdad there were barrage balloons floating over the city. In Beirut, I initially found the airport security faintly amusing, only to understand its seriousness when John McCarthy and Terry Waite were kidnapped a few weeks later.

I enjoyed almost every minute of it. I did it my way.

Chapter 1 — Starting Work

On Monday, 6 July 1964, I turned fifteen. Eighteen days later, on Friday, 24 July, my school broke up for the summer recess. Unlike every summer before it, I walked home that day knowing — although not fully realising — that it would be for the last time. I would never again sit in a classroom with the people I had spent the previous four years alongside. At fifteen years and eighteen days old, excited to no longer be a schoolboy and wholly unprepared, I stepped out into the wider world.

I was the son of a miner, brought up in the close-knit community of a mining village. Locally, employment options were limited. The National Coal Board dominated the area, advertising *Jobs for Life* on billboards everywhere. Three pits — Allerton Bywater, Primrose Hill, and Ledston Luck — together with their regional North Yorkshire headquarters, lay within two miles of where I lived.

Despite this, neither my mother nor my father wanted any of their children to follow him down the pit.

My eldest brother, Laurie, had begun as a mining engineer-fitter but by 1964 had already acquired his own garage on York Road in Leeds. My sister Joan and her husband both worked at the Yorkshire Copper Works. My second eldest brother, Graham, was training as an architect, and my younger brother, Stephen, worked for Laurie. When it came time for me to choose, I followed my sister to the Copper Works.

The Yorkshire Copper Works had already merged with the metals division of ICI and become Yorkshire Imperial Metals

The Export Adventurer

Limited, though almost everyone still referred to it simply as "the Copper Works".

On Monday, 27 July 1964, I reported for my first job, in the mailroom. My starting pay was £3 11s 1d — £3.56 per week — for hours of 8:30 to 12:45 and 1:45 to 5:00, a 37½-hour week.

Mr Wade, the apprentice training officer, conducted the induction for all new starters under eighteen. There were three of us: two beginning works apprenticeships, and one in a suit — me. He outlined the training programmes, explained that we would attend further education one day a week, and described the support available. I enrolled at Whitwood Technical College to study Economic History and Commerce.

The company provided a bus pass or reimbursed fares to and from work and college, and until the age of eighteen we were given vouchers for free meals in the canteen. The bus pass also proved useful on Saturdays, as I joined the Yorkshire Copper Works rugby team. The induction ended with a tour of the offices, factory and canteen — and a cup of tea.

The site itself was enormous — perhaps a square kilometre or more. Alongside the mills, service buildings and laboratories, the canteen complex stood out. One large building housed an always-open works canteen with a long counter serving sandwiches, pies, tea and coffee. Beside it was a bar serving Tetley's beer. Upstairs was a smaller staff canteen with waitress service, and beyond that, separate dining rooms for executives and directors.

The Copper Works functioned almost as a self-contained township. It had its own fire engine, a medical centre with a private ambulance, payphones, and even its own bus station — created by converting a car park. Arrangements were made with the West Riding Automobile Company to run evening routes to surrounding districts, including one stopping within a hundred yards of my home.

That afternoon, after completing my bus pass application and receiving a month's supply of blue tickets for free lunches, I was taken to the mailroom and introduced to Jack Smith, the manager, and Peter Darling, his assistant. The mailroom staff distributed internal mail, packed parcels — literature, samples, anything that needed sending — and acted as general gofers. If something needed moving anywhere across the office or factory complex, we did it. Jack and Peter were both thoroughly decent people, and it was through Jack that I joined the rugby team.

Placing new young employees in the mailroom was inspired. It allowed us to find our feet among people of our own age and acted as a bridge between school and working life. Delivering mail gave insight into the breadth of departments: Circularising, Purchasing, COIP — whatever that was — Home Sales, Export, Marketing, Computers, Wages, Cashiers, Accounts, Costs, Stationery Supplies, Samples, Printing, Metal Buying, Production Control, and even a Calculating Department, known as Comptometers. Job vacancies were posted on noticeboards; it was only a matter of time before something interesting appeared.

The Copper Works looked after its female staff just as well, placing them in the Teleprinter Room, handling all telex communications in the days before fax and email. Twice daily, a canteen worker arrived with a trolley of hot water urns and set up a booth. Each department sent down a junior to collect tea and coffee in plastic cups.

Profits from the canteen bar funded sports facilities, supporting rugby, cricket, football, tennis and numerous other clubs. Although the rugby union team was sometimes dismissed as a "works side" by old-boys' clubs, we never paid for kit or laundry.

Tennis courts were available, equipment loaned freely, and this generosity extended across all sports.

Every weekday at 12:45, we marched to the canteen for a free, well-cooked roast dinner, followed by a traditional pudding. The only drawback was plastic cutlery, so most of us carried our own knives and forks — often tucked into suit jacket pockets alongside red and blue Bic pens.

At fifteen and a half, I decided I fancied handling cash and applied for a position in the Cashiers Department. I assisted Frank Taylor, Barry Eaton and Tom Wilkinson, paying weekly wages to Group 3 staff and reimbursing expenses from petty cash. It was repetitive work, and after a couple of years I realised I could never be a bean counter.

(Above, L to r). M. Heathcote, G. Bratley, M. Wrigglesworth, members of the Leeds Works Rugby Club who have been selected for the Inter District Trials.

I discussed this with Frank. It was he who first suggested that export was the future.

The Export Adventurer

What began as a first job in a mailroom would soon pull me beyond factory walls and national borders, into a world where trade, politics and risk were inseparable.

Chapter 2 — The 'Copper Works' (Yorkshire Imperial Metals Limited)

Export Department

On Monday, 26 June 1967, I walked into the Export Department at the 'Copper Works'.

Export did not inhabit a purpose-built office block with plate glass and carpeting. It lived in an old, converted, single-storey engineering mill — an industrial space pressed into administrative service. The roof was a saw-tooth pitch, like a series of triangular garden cloches: Georgian wired glass on one side and corrugated steel sheets on the other. The arrangement had one main virtue — it kept the weather out. Its side effects were less kind. In sunshine the place became a greenhouse; in winter, with little insulation, it developed the crisp atmosphere of a refrigerated aisle.

Inside, it was a mix of the newly painted and the unmistakably antique. The floor was dark solid parquet throughout. Wooden stud partitions, painted in various shades of grey, broke the mill into a central open-plan area with a ring of small offices around it — rooms for senior managers, regional sales representatives, and the typing pool. Frosted glass windows gave you silhouettes and movement but not much privacy, which was probably for the best, as it discouraged anyone from thinking they could have a quiet life.

The Export Adventurer

The furniture did most of the time-travelling. The desks were ancient dark oak and arranged in fan shapes around a central pedestal containing the electrical sockets. Power ran up from there through two or three round metal conduits suspended overhead, linking back to the main supply. No fancy "boss", no decorative flourish — just practical electrics doing their best in a building with a previous life. The chairs, in contrast, were relatively modern wheeled swivel chairs. The walls were freshly painted but bare, except for the occasional freight forwarder's calendar. The overall impression was of antiquity being asked to keep up.

The open-plan area was divided into four principal sub-departments: Orders, Invoicing, Shipping, and the section I was joining — Export Quotations. In total, there were about fifty people in Export: eight to ten in each main section, about half a dozen regional export sales managers, two responsible for filing and statistics, and somewhere between fifteen and twenty in the typing pool. With today's computerisation, I suspect four to six people could cope with the workload — though they would miss the character-building experience of sending paper on a grand tour of the mill.

On my first day, I was introduced to everyone in Export Quotations and then spent the afternoon with a colleague, Jim Butterick, who showed me the basics of what was, at the time, an alarming and mind-boggling administrative process.

Years later I realised I had been looking at something quietly exceptional. The 'Copper Works' export system had been developed over time into a set-but-flexible method that processed everything in a disciplined way without becoming brittle. Everyone knew their role. Everyone did it properly. The trick was not simply following rules — it was knowing when to bend them without breaking anything.

The information system

In those days, you could not search a database. You consulted a book.

There was an international trade guide — Croner's — available on subscription, which listed the rules and regulations for shipping goods into every country. Updates arrived regularly, because the world has always enjoyed changing its mind. The Export Quotations Department took this A5 loose-leaf guide, split it up, and filed each page into foolscap binders (the paper size before A4). They then added the company's own national instructions for each country, creating a centralised information resource long before anyone talked about "systems".

That resource mattered because the details were not decorative. Southern Rhodesia, for example, following the Unilateral Declaration of Independence, was embargoed; there was no point quoting at all. Australia, meanwhile, was — and remains — hyper-vigilant about preventing foreign bugs and viruses entering the country. Straw and chaff packaging were banned entirely because they might harbour vermin or insects. Then you added the requirements of your overseas agent: perhaps two copies of everything — one for the local office and one for head office. Multiply this by dozens

The Export Adventurer

of countries and you could either organise it properly or collapse into paperwork.

The binder was kept meticulously up to date. For each enquiry, essential information was transferred onto a yellow A5 glued-edge label attached to the bottom of the original letter or telex. That label carried country instructions and also had boxes for management guidance — pricing, delivery expectations from production, clauses required by the typing pool, and so on. It was brilliant. Computers have made it easier, but the principle remains the same: in international trade, organisation is not tidiness — it is survival.

Work on your feet

In those days, people were on their feet much of the time. Almost every enquiry differed: size, copper alloy, length, finish, and any number of other variables. We dealt with ship pipelines and condenser tubes, plumbing tubes and fittings, medical gas lines, tubeplates, and bimetal finned tubing.

Each enquiry also had to be physically circulated. It went to Costs for production costs, to Production for a delivery forecast, to Shipping for freight rates, and finally to the Export Quotations manager for margin and payment term instructions. Paper travelled more than some employees.

And because the work was detailed — and mistakes were expensive — having your calculations checked was not optional.

Calculations

Pricing copper alloy tube could be quite complex. First you took the London Metal Exchange price of the metals making

The Export Adventurer

up the alloy — copper, zinc, nickel, aluminium, and so on. Then you added the cost of producing the tube from raw materials (the conversion cost) to establish product cost. Then you added export delivery costs such as packing, freight, and marine insurance. All of this was done in old pence per pound.

In 1967 there were no electronic calculators — only mechanical machines such as the Swedish Odhner. If you wanted to calculate 15.87 multiplied by twenty-one, you entered 15.87 into the machine and wound the handle twenty-one times until the answer appeared. The machine would dutifully provide digits but offered no assistance whatsoever in locating the decimal point. That part was left to your brain. It was a wonderful way of discovering who had been paying attention in maths.

The 'Copper Works' also had a calculating department — "Comptometers" — where about twenty girls used mechanical, push-button Sumlock calculators. Even with that support, the process seems almost unbelievable now: write the calculations in formula format, send them to another department, and wait for the results to be returned. But that was normal. And because it was normal, it had to be checked.

Correspondence

Most correspondence was done by telex — teleprinter messages sent over telephone lines and printed at the recipient's end. Where customers did not have those facilities, letters went by post.

That usually meant drafting longhand. Dictaphones existed, but they were in short supply and usually already in use, so obtaining one could become a small competitive sport. Drafts and/or recordings went to the typing pool, where letters were typed on mechanical typewriters. Errors could sometimes be scratched out with a razor blade or painted over with Tippex; otherwise, they were retyped. The Dictaphone itself resembled an oatmeal-coloured record player with a microphone and a matching long-playing record — an object that somehow managed to look both harmless and authoritative.

I still remember one evening working overtime when someone was dictating into a Dictaphone in an outrageous imitation of Jomo Kenyatta, producing a letter of such magnificence that the rest of us were helpless. At that moment, a stern security man — ex-police by manner if not by badge — walked through the door, paused, and said only, "Enjoying yourselves?" Then he left. We stopped laughing instantly and returned to work with the diligence of children caught mid-mischief. It was so like being at school that you almost expected a bell.

The world arrives on your desk

Export is where global events stop being headlines and start being costs.

The 1967 Arab–Israeli Six-Day War closed the Suez Canal, and shipping companies increased freight rates by 12.5% because vessels had to go around the Cape of Good Hope. Suez later reopened, but the Cape surcharge was absorbed into freight rates long ago and — somehow — never quite went away.

1973 was probably the most turbulent peacetime year I experienced in export. Harold Wilson devalued the pound from $2.80 to $2.40 — one penny effectively equating to one cent. Meanwhile, the copper supply situation was already complicated. Ian Smith's Unilateral Declaration of Independence in Southern Rhodesia on 11 November 1965 was critical because Zambian copper could no longer be shipped out through the embargoed Rhodesian railway system. Then, in 1973, Chile — then the largest copper producer in the world — went into civil war. Copper prices rose so high that the scrap value of an old penny exceeded its face value.

During the second Arab–Israeli war in 1973, I also learned that commerce does not wait for peace. I had two orders on my desk for pricing at the same time: one for medical gas lines and fittings from the Aleppo Hospital Committee, and the other for shell bands for the Ministry of Defence in Tel Aviv.

Metrication and the home market surprise

I stayed with the 'Copper Works' for nine years and witnessed the first major event in British–Continental European integration: metrication.

The shilling disappeared. We began quoting in pounds per 100 kg instead of pence per pound. When plumbing metricated in 1971, part of our home market disappeared. We assumed that moving from ½-inch nominal size BS659 copper pipe to the new shiny metric 15mm OD BS2871 would allow us to attack the French, German and Swedish markets, because they too used 15mm OD in their plumbing standards.

Alas, we were mistaken. On D-Day, Svenska Metalverken already held the British Standard Kitemark for BS2871 and had stock in Hull. We were being attacked in our own backyard and not enjoying the opportunities metrication had promised.

To their credit, management had prepared. Western European plumbing sales were transferred to a new department, the Western European Sales Office (WESO), under the guidance of a manager who ran it dynamically and used modern marketing techniques to penetrate Western Europe. Whether that compensated for the loss of the home market is another question.

In Export, we could see the satisfying rise in overseas sales, but we were largely unaware of the damage that losing part of the UK market was doing to the business overall.

A sideways "promotion"

After two or three years in Export Quotations, I was given extra duties assisting a Regional Export Manager. I was proud of what I saw as a promotion. In truth, it was a sideways move: I carried on doing my own job and also became his gofer, with no mention of a pay rise.

His markets were the Republic of Ireland and the Caribbean. I scanned trade magazines and architects' journals for announcements of projects, and he pursued them through consultants, architects, contractors and project owners. Even now, I still recall sales of plumbing tubes and fittings into developments in Montego Bay, Jamaica.

The annealed tubes letter

One day we received a letter from a regular client in the sugar industry, who had bought numerous 70/30 brass condenser tubes.

These tubes were fixed into pre-drilled threaded holes in a tubeplate at each end of a boiler. At one end, access allowed a compression ferrule assembly. At the other — at the blind end — access was limited or non-existent. In such cases, the tubes were annealed (softened) at the factory before dispatch, allowing a small explosive charge to be fitted into the annealed blind end during assembly. On detonation, the tube expanded into position.

The client informed us that we had annealed the wrong end.

A Regional Export Manager and I spent the best part of an afternoon trying to find the correct syntax to tell them, politely and without offence, to turn the tubes around. It was less a technical problem than a diplomatic one.

Social life and the mill's sense of humour

Tea and coffee from the tea trolley were perfectly acceptable, provided you drank them exactly when the tea trolley was present. Outside those times, you had to use a vending machine, which reliably produced something hot and brown but rarely something you would actively choose. So we bought a coffee percolator. The resulting coffee was so popular that even one or two export managers quietly bought theirs from us.

Someone brought in Subbuteo and the green baize pitch. The baize would not sit flat on desk tops, so we mounted it on hardboard and created proper playing surfaces. Several people bought sets, we formed a league, and later added a rugby Subbuteo league as well. Four or five pitches were stored in corners during the day and brought out at lunchtime for scheduled league and cup matches. There were cups. It became serious enough that it probably deserved its own compliance department.

We ran a Littlewoods Pools syndicate, and I ran a "buster": the first team to score eleven cumulative goals won; if you went past it, you went bust. At one point over forty people participated. When a relatively new starter was invited to join the buster, coffee and pools syndicates, he responded: "I'll be in anything bar an excrement sandwich, because I don't like bread."

There was also an under-the-counter book club where half a dozen of us contributed to costs and took turns to borrow the book. That extra "education" undoubtedly improved imaginations and may have increased the number of dependants in the long term.

Sport ran through the culture as well: rugby, football, cricket, tennis and golf competitions each summer. Departments formed teams for inter-department knockouts. There was an annual open day on the sports fields, with refreshments, free roundabouts and bouncy castles for families.

If you were sick or injured, Personnel had welfare staff who visited, delivered wages, and often arranged loans or grants to help people cope. It was, for all its industrial rough edges, a company that looked after its own.

Nights out were frequent, especially in Wakefield: Yates's Wine Lodge, then the Beer Keller, finishing with fish and chips in a basket at Heppy's.

One night in Leeds, a colleague arrived late in a very smart new trench coat and asked someone with a distinctive maroon Riley Hornet if he could place the coat in the car boot. The boot was said to be unlocked, so the coat was stored. At closing time, we walked out and the coat owner anxiously announced someone had stolen the car. The car owner simply pointed to the far corner of the car park and said, "No they haven't — my car is over there."

Another evening, working late, there was a commotion in Export Shipping: a wastepaper bin had burst into flames. One person was on the second drag of a freshly lit cigarette, while another was stamping out the fire. Unfortunately, a coat was hanging above the bin and the flames charred the side and arm. Once the fire was out, the owner brought the coat to a senior manager with a view to making a claim. The senior manager examined it and said, "Can't you get it invisibly mended?"

The Export Adventurer

The roof produced its own entertainment. With the glass and corrugated sheets, the office could become unbearable in sunshine. After a lunchtime cricket session on a sweltering day, everyone returned in shirtsleeves. One chap had football shorts with him and changed in the toilets, then crept back and hid his bare legs under the desk. While he wasn't looking, someone removed and hid his trousers. He began asking, "Come on — who's taken my trousers?" A few minutes later, the tannoy announced: "Will anyone finding a pair of trousers please return them to Malcolm Robinson in the Export Department."

Cricket produced another episode involving a stream running along the boundary, a scoreboard accessed by a purpose-built bridge, and a culvert under the road offering a second crossing point within twenty yards. Someone hit a six and the ball landed on a mud bank across the stream. Rather than walk ten yards left to the bridge or ten yards right to the culvert, the fielder attempted to jump onto the mud bank to save time. His feet sank and kept sinking until he was waist deep in black, slimy, decomposing organic mud. The smell was horrific. It was also time to return to work. All the way back, he scraped at his legs and trousers, repeating over and over: "effing bastard mud."

On the last day before Christmas, it was tradition to clear desks by lunchtime and go to the Stepping Stones for drinks, drifting back mid-afternoon slightly inebriated. The interactions between the mailroom, teleprinter room and the younger office staff became legendary. There was not a broom cupboard, muniment room or cloakroom that didn't see some activity that afternoon. Even now, it amazes me how lenient senior management was on that one particular day.

Looking back

In those days, Yorkshire Copper Works was regarded as the best company in the Leeds area for commercial and office training. I look back with nostalgic pleasure. The people were not merely colleagues; they were a community. Fifty years on, I still meet up monthly with four or five ex-'Copper Works' colleagues, and at Christmas we hold a get-together attended by around thirty. I am clearly not the only one who carries the place fondly.

The company was technologically at the top of its tree at the time, and its systems and practices were second to none. My own versions of them served me throughout my career. Many of the characters from those years are no longer with us.

In Export, it was rewarding to see sales increasing through Western European plumbing sales, but we did not fully see the adverse effects that losing part of the UK market was having on the business overall. The metals division of ICI skimmed off profits, leaving little for reinvestment. Manufacturing methods that had once been cutting-edge became antiquated, outdated and expensive, and eventually succumbed to more modern technology elsewhere.

The 'Copper Works' (Yorkshire Imperial Metals Limited) went from employing thousands at its headquarters and factory in Leeds — with a tubeplates factory in Landore, tube and pipe factories in Kirkby (Liverpool) and Smethwick (Birmingham), and a fittings factory in Dundee — into decline, finally closing its doors in 1998.

Since then, much of our manufacturing has disappeared. We now buy many manufactured products from abroad, and much of our water and electricity is invoiced to us by German and French companies.

What I learned at the 'Copper Works' — about systems, people, diplomacy and unintended consequences — would shape everything that followed, as my working life moved beyond a single company and into government, trade promotion and the wider world.

Chapter 3 — Marriage and Serious Money

In 1968, on 10 February, I got married. My wife and I bought a two-bedroom terraced house with a bathroom, a large dining kitchen, and another generous reception room.

A local builder had already divided one of the bedrooms into two to create space for a bathroom. Unfortunately for him — and very fortunately for us — he ran into other pressures, failed to finish the job, and had no time to return. His incapacity allowed us to buy the house at the knockdown price of £950. I was under twenty-one, so my parents acted as guarantors, and Bradford Permanent Building Society granted us a mortgage repayable at £6 0s 4d per month.

Over the next three years, we had three children in quick succession.

My income from the 'Copper Works' was enough to keep us going but left nothing spare for luxuries, so I looked for ways to supplement it. On Sundays I worked for a local poultry farmer, maintaining his chicken sheds. He had six thousand laying hens housed in long battery pens in ageing wooden huts, and there was always something broken, loose, or blown off in the wind that needed repairing.

Around us were other young couples with small children. One neighbour, a close friend, had an allotment — mainly for his pigeons, but also to grow vegetables for his family. I applied for an allotment myself, about a hundred yards from our front door. Unlike my friend, who did just enough to meet the conditions, I threw myself into it. I grew more than we could eat and sold the excess to neighbours and colleagues at work.

In time I built a chicken shed from reclaimed timber. Eggs and vegetables supplemented our table and added a little to our income.

Once the work inside the house was finished, I turned my attention outside. Each house had a red-brick, slate-roofed block containing a toilet, a coal house, and a bin store, all opening onto a shared yard of compacted earth and ash. With the neighbours' agreement — and help — we demolished the outbuildings, laid the bricks over the ground, poured an inch or two of concrete, and divided the area into individually fenced back gardens. For the first time, everyone had somewhere safe for their children to play.

Square onions and eggs

Around this time there was a television advert for Kraft cheese slices. The sandwich was assembled with impressive geometric discipline: square bread, square cheese, square onion, square egg. One of the lads in Export Quotes remarked how stupid it was to suggest you could get square onions and eggs.

I decided to prove him wrong.

Near my home there was a poultry farm where the hens were kept in battery cages. The farmer's son was a friend of mine, and whenever I called at his house, I was usually sent away laden with cracked and soft-shelled eggs — far more than any normal household could sensibly use. Chickens kept in cages cannot forage for grit and minerals, so they rely entirely on their feed to form eggshells, and occasionally that process goes awry. Almost every visit resulted in a carrier bag full of eggs with membranes but no hard shell.

That solved half the problem.

I made a three-inch square wooden box with no top or bottom and slid it over a growing onion on my allotment. A month later the onion had obligingly grown to the shape of the box. I then made a smaller square box, carefully eased a soft-shelled egg into it, and boiled it until it hardened.

Armed with a square onion and a square egg, I arrived at work and made my colleague his sandwich. His astonishment was deeply satisfying, and the advert was never mentioned again.

Bratley Newton Associates

By the summer of 1972 the government launched a grant-backed programme to modernise old houses. The problem was tradespeople: the building industry was already overwhelmed.

At the same time, almost every household wanted plumbing installed for automatic washing machines. I had already done a few minor plumbing jobs at home and began taking on small projects for friends, relatives, and colleagues.

A colleague became interested in another idea I was considering: breeding pigs. I needed capital; he was keen. We chose a vacant allotment near mine and named the venture Bratley Newton Associates — a name I would use for the next seven years.

We visited the Great Yorkshire Show in Harrogate to look at pig-farrowing equipment. While there, we attempted to discuss insurance with various companies, but they were far more interested in supplying us with free gin and tonics, cream teas, and sandwiches. Once we had reached the point where

The Export Adventurer

we could consume no more, a cloudburst drove us onto a French bus serving Pernod cocktails, where we waited out the rain in good spirits.

We bought one gilt in pig, which produced eight piglets. We raised them to slaughter, then jointly decided pig breeding was not for us. The partnership ended amicably. At least we had tried.

By the early 1970s, I was learning that the only reliable way to get ahead was to improvise — and that the best opportunities often arrived disguised as hard work, side projects, and sheer cheek.

Chapter 4 — BNA-Gowanbury Limited

The turning point came with an enquiry from Kuwait.

At the 'Copper Works' I was still supplying plumbing tubes and fittings to all countries outside Western Europe. British architects and consultants were designing hospitals, hotels and commercial buildings across the Middle East. My job was to extract the copper elements from the specifications and prepare quotations, usually accompanied by a polite letter explaining that we did not manufacture the rest.

On one occasion, a customer in Kuwait wrote back asking — almost pleading — for help identifying the other manufacturers.

I took the enquiry home and borrowed *Kelly's Manufacturers and Merchants Directory* from the local library.

Operating as Bratley Newton Associates, I contacted British manufacturers of electrical and mechanical services: cables, cable trays, conduit, sockets and switches, valves, sanitary ware, baths and more. I assembled quotations for everything, added 5 per cent, and sent off a professional-looking offer.

Three weeks later an envelope arrived from Lloyds Bank in London containing a letter of credit for £112,000. The project was the Kuwait water towers; the contractor was Abdul Razak.

At the time my salary at the 'Copper Works' was £1,750 per annum. My 5 per cent margin on that single order came to £5,600.

The Export Adventurer

That was when I realised this was no longer a sideline.

I bought an off-the-shelf limited company, Gowanbury Limited, changed its name to **BNA-Gowanbury Limited**, and set off in earnest.

Once the company existed, opportunities appeared everywhere.

I began by reviewing enquiries that the 'Copper Works' had turned away and quickly identified several with real potential. My next contract was with an Iranian government corporation for steel tubes, which I sourced from the Japanese company Toyo Menka. It confirmed what I had suspected: there was plenty of business available if you were prepared to assemble it rather than manufacture it.

The next question was how to find more clients.

That question answered itself when I spoke with a Lebanese import–export merchant based in London. He specialised in supplying material packages for large hotels across the Middle East. I already knew most of the electrical and mechanical services manufacturers; he had access to contractors and projects. We agreed — correctly — that cooperation would benefit us both.

His expertise lay in large hotel kitchens and housekeeping equipment. He operated from a mews apartment in Knightsbridge and spent much of his time in Beirut dealing with formidable Lebanese contractors. Based on my track record, he was convinced the arrangement would work.

Leaving the Copper Works

This brought me to a crossroads.

Up to that point I had operated BNA-Gowanbury in my spare time — evenings and weekends. Working from London meant severing my lifeline with the 'Copper Works'. Weekly travel would also disrupt family life.

Looking back, I have to admit that part of the attraction was London itself — the big smoke exerted more pull than it probably should have. In the end, I resigned from the 'Copper Works', and offices were leased on the second floor of 65 Knightsbridge.

Our first joint project was the Aqaba Holiday Inn. His company supplied kitchens and much of the housekeeping equipment; BNA-Gowanbury Limited supplied all the mechanical (plumbing) and electrical materials.

The partnership lasted around two years. It worked well, but eventually we decided to go our separate ways. I moved into modest offices above a barbershop in my home town of Castleford.

What I took with me was not just experience, but method. He had taught me the art of prospecting — how to spot a project early, how to follow it, and when to commit.

Big projects and bigger trust

Over the next four or five years, BNA-Gowanbury supplied projects including Salmaniya Medical Centre in Bahrain and Salalah Hospital in Muscat.

The Export Adventurer

For Salalah, the main supplier requested a transferable and divisible irrevocable confirmed letter of credit. When I asked for it, they suggested something simpler: sending the cash up front.

With a contract value exceeding £300,000, this was a leap of trust I had not expected.

One requirement was £30,000 worth of copper tubes and fittings, which I placed with my former employer, the 'Copper Works'. Shortly afterwards I was invited to a meeting. They explained, apologetically, that they did not believe BNA-Gowanbury had the means to pay.

With the full contract value already sitting in the bank, I offered to prepay and wrote the cheque. The expressions on their faces as I handed it over remain unforgettable. I am sure the cheque was banked immediately — and that the confirmation caused further surprise.

On another occasion, a Middle Eastern client asked me to act as a buying agent for a 5 per cent commission, with letters of credit opened directly in favour of the suppliers — including my markup.

This meant asking suppliers to inflate their prices by 5 per cent and reimburse me once they had been paid. Anyone who declined simply did not receive an order.

One supplier was, again, the 'Copper Works'. After shipment and payment they reimbursed me around £5,000. Just eighteen months earlier I had worked for them full-time for £1,750 per year. Fate arranged that when I collected the cheque, it was handed to me by my former manager, now promoted to chief cashier.

Turning specifications to advantage

Most projects were built to specifications written by British consultants, who almost always used the phrase *"manufactured by XYZ or equal"*.

That phrase was gold.

Many manufacturers did not actually manufacture everything they sold. One famous bathroom supplier produced its porcelain items — basins, toilets and cisterns — in Scotland, but bought in taps, brassware and steel baths from elsewhere, adding substantial margins.

By buying the porcelain from them and sourcing everything else directly from the true manufacturers, we could offer an identical technical package at prices they could not match. If they raised prices, we simply invoked the *"or equal"* clause and bought from another British manufacturer producing to the same standards.

At one point the situation became so acute that the supplier asked us not to quote for the sanitary ware on a prestige project and offered £5,000 in return. We agreed — while supplying everything else.

Logistics at scale

Salalah Hospital involved hundreds of thousands of items across thousands of product lines. Everything had to be containerised.

Two items dominated the shipping: one hundred tonnes of sheet steel for air-conditioning ducting and 4,000 cubic metres of rock-wool insulation.

Steel hit weight limits long before volume; insulation hit volume long before weight. The solution was simple: ten inches of steel on the container floor — about sixteen tonnes — with insulation stacked above.

That required bringing insulation from Denmark to the UK, combining it with UK-produced steel, finding a freight forwarder in Hull with storage and container-stuffing facilities, and persuading P&O to divert one of their *Strath* vessels to Hull.

The insulation came by barge from Esbjerg. Containers arrived from multiple suppliers. The forwarder topped them up and merged loads.

In the end, there was so much cargo that P&O scheduled a special sailing. *Strathclyde* sailed directly from Hull to Muscat carrying nothing but our goods.

They later invited my wife and me to their Christmas dinner at the Queen's Hotel in Leeds. After dinner, drinks arrived by the bottle, cigars were lit on request, and spare cigars were left on the table "just in case".

It was an evening that felt far removed from square onions.

Success, missteps and consequences

Business was exceedingly good. We moved from our terraced house to a modern townhouse, then to a large semi-detached home. Holidays followed — caravanning in the UK, trips to France and Spain, and city breaks to London, Paris and Lisbon.

The only real misstep came via an introduced associate who claimed strong connections. His expenses far exceeded his usefulness. After he left, the police appeared. They had arrested him for theft from another employer and discovered he had taken photocopies of our correspondence.

To protect the company's reputation, I agreed to prosecute. The trial lasted three days. I spent a full day in the witness box and eventually demonstrated the absurdity of the defence claim that I had forced him to carry a suitcase of documents home. The jury laughed; the judge smiled; the defence sat down.

After the guilty verdict, I asked the police to destroy the files. We had the originals.

Bahrain and beyond

After that episode I returned to business travel — Lebanon, Jordan, Bahrain and the Emirates. I secured several large orders, including welders, safety equipment and infrastructure materials.

One order stood out. I arrived unannounced at a contractor's office just as two overdressed British salesmen were being shown out. I was ushered straight in. Later I learned why: the owner valued practicality. If you could not dress sensibly for the climate, he would not waste time listening to you.

I looked down at my safari shirt, beige chinos and desert boots and silently approved of my choices.

In Bahrain I spent six months based near Budaiya, living alone while the family remained in the UK. Life was comfortable, if

The Export Adventurer

lonely. The British Club, hotel bars full of expatriate engineers, and chance encounters with entertainers provided company.

On one flight home, an airline engineer casually listed faults on the aircraft I was about to board — adding cheerfully that all systems had backups. I do not think I would accept that reassurance quite so calmly today.

Bahrain

Eventually my clients grew sophisticated enough to employ their own buyers. My days of quietly adding 5 per cent came to an end.

The education remained.

Those years taught me more about people, trust, improvisation and international trade than any formal training ever could. Like the square onion, it was all about understanding constraints — and shaping solutions to fit them.

It was good while it lasted.

By the mid-1970s, the lessons were no longer about how to build a business — but about how long momentum, trust and good fortune can be relied upon before something has to change.

Chapter 5 — Italrad

As the BNA business began to decline, I started looking around for other opportunities. One arrived unexpectedly, following an enquiry to supply central-heating equipment for a project in Syria.

The radiators specified were the old cast-iron neoclassical type, the sort commonly found in schools and public buildings. By then, only one UK manufacturer still produced them, which gave that company a comfortable price monopoly. We began looking internationally for alternatives and eventually found a company in northern Italy manufacturing a similar system in aluminium, but with far more modern styling.

Aluminium has significantly higher thermal conductivity than cast iron, so each radiator section produced a higher heat output. As a result, the radiators could be smaller, narrower and far less intrusive.

We sent samples to both the project owners and the consulting engineers, who were more than happy to amend the specification to aluminium. Each section was approximately 50 mm wide and available in various heights. A 600 mm section delivered around 650 BTUs, meaning an aluminium radiator could occupy roughly a third of the wall space of its cast-iron equivalent.

That chance enquiry marked the start of a long relationship with the manufacturers in Modena.

Forming Italrad

Together with a friend who was coming to the end of a long contract with a Swiss–Liechtenstein boiler manufacturer, we decided to take on the exclusive distributorship for the aluminium radiators in the UK. We formed a new company: **Italrad Limited**.

My partner took responsibility for UK sales and proved extremely effective. Before long, one of the UK's largest national plumbing and heating merchants was selling our products through all of its branches.

We set up a workshop in Castleford where we assembled radiators to the required sizes and outputs. As business grew, visits to Modena became frequent. Travelling by car was far more economical than flying, and in those days we were young enough not to worry too much about comfort.

European road trips

We would leave early in the morning, cross the Channel, and avoid French motorway tolls by travelling through Belgium, France, Germany and Switzerland. The only toll we ever paid was on the short Metz–Strasbourg section.

On one trip our office manager accompanied me. To avoid seasonal snow via the Simplon Pass, we chose an alternative route. Naturally, it snowed heavily, and we ended up taking the car train through the Alps. Descending onto the northern Italian plains, the brakes began to feel disturbingly spongy. We reached our hotel in Modena with my hair standing on end.

The following morning I mentioned the brakes to our hosts. They took the keys and whisked the car away. When we returned that evening, the car was back in the hotel car park with a note on Ferrari factory notepaper explaining that all the rubber seals in the brake callipers had been replaced. One had been leaking.

It transpired that the radiator company's CEO had a brother who was a senior engineer at Ferrari.

On the return journey we went via Mont Blanc, through the 15-kilometre tunnel, down through Chamonix and back into France. It was challenging enough that I reverted permanently to my original route: Lille, Metz, Strasbourg, Basel and Lucerne.

On one trip my father accompanied me as co-driver. As we sped down the German autobahn between Strasbourg and Basel, he remarked that we had been passing a town unfamiliar to him for some time. I asked its name.

"Ausfahrt," he replied.

Fuel, favours and funerals

I always left the UK with a full tank, as fuel was more expensive on the continent. In Italy, however, we exploited the tourist fuel-coupon system, buying coupons at half price from the Italian AA, filling the tank, and selling the unused coupons at a profit.

Once we received an order for two radiators so large that transporting them assembled was impractical. My brother-in-law and I took the sections to Barnsley Crematorium and assembled them on site. Forty years later, when I attended a funeral there in 2016, I was delighted to see both radiators still in service.

Alloy wheels and Italian strikes

The radiator factory belonged to a group headquartered in Bergamo that also manufactured alloy wheels. I expressed interest, and we were offered the distributorship.

On my first visit, I arrived near Como with an almost empty fuel tank. All the filling stations were closed — later I learned there was a nationwide strike. The gauge dropped steadily until I was convinced we would grind to a halt.

I spotted two police officers on motorbikes, indicated my predicament, and they motioned for me to follow them. They led me through tiny roads to a village filling station with hand-cranked pumps. Rather than offer money, I gave them a few King Edward cigars each, which they accepted happily.

After meetings in Bergamo, my father and I realised we had time to visit Venice. It took longer than expected. We spent several hours there, including a coffee in St Mark's Square accompanied by a full orchestra. When the bill arrived, my father was outraged. When I explained that the price included the music, he replied:

"Tell them not to charge me. I'm not listening."

Finding our way back to the car was pure guesswork. By luck rather than judgement, we boarded the correct water bus.

On the return journey, after driving from Italy to Folkestone and landing at 10 pm, we were stopped by a policeman in Castleford at 3 am, two miles from home. When I told him we had come from Italy, he looked at the clothes hanging in the back and said, "You haven't hung around."

"No," I replied. "I've driven like this all the way."

Success — and saturation

The alloy wheels were astonishingly easy to sell. Their design closely resembled the famous Minilites used on Monte Carlo Minis. Demand was immediate and widespread.

Within a few years, however, every distributor and stockist who wanted them already had them. Sales narrowed to small quantities for niche vehicles. We had been too successful for our own longevity.

Although the radiator business continued to grow, it was not growing fast enough to replace the declining income from BNA-Gowanbury or the now-saturated alloy-wheel trade.

I decided to step back from running my own businesses. I transferred my shares in Italrad to my partner, who took the business to our principal customer and became their employee.

I joined Marley Extrusions as a Sales Representative.

It was time for the next chapter.

For the first time in years, I was returning not to entrepreneurship, but to employment — taking with me everything that self-employment had taught me.

Chapter 6 — Marley Extrusions

On 1 April 1979, at 8:30 in the morning, I was collected from home by Alan Kent — who always introduced himself as "Kent with an E" — and transported to Harrogate, the North-East headquarters of Marley Extrusions Limited. It was my first day in a new job as Underground Drainage Representative for Yorkshire and North Lincolnshire.

I remember wondering, not entirely cheerfully, how I would cope after seven years of making my own decisions. Now I would be expected to follow instructions from Marley management: a branch manager, Tom Allerdice, and two assistant managers, Peter Woodhouse and Alan Kent.

The induction day was largely administration and reporting — forms, procedures, expectations, and the subtle art of looking busy while learning where the toilets were. Mid-afternoon, another new representative and I were whisked away to a Marley Tile factory in Durham to collect the cars allocated to us. We had been told to expect a basic Vauxhall Cavalier or Ford Cortina, but we had no idea whether we were receiving new vehicles or ones that had already lived a previous life.

On arrival, we were taken straight to the transport manager. Paperwork was signed. We were issued Shell and All-Star fuel credit cards — an early sign that Marley took mileage very seriously — and then we were shown to our vehicles.

We were both elated. Two brand-new, gleaming Vauxhall Cavaliers: one powder blue, one canary yellow. My car was the powder blue one — HKR 676V — with only delivery mileage on the clock. My teatime drive home from Durham was extremely pleasant.

The Export Adventurer

The rest of the week was taken up with product training in Harrogate, followed by a full week at Marley's headquarters near Maidstone. The training was excellent. Even now I can still calculate how deep a drain will be, given the correct information — one of those skills you don't often need socially, but which never quite leaves you.

The salary was reasonable and there was a bonus scheme if you could beat the previous year's sales figures. Unfortunately, 1979 and 1980 were recession years in construction, and sales were generally slow.

Still, I found gold in the Vale of York.

The Vale is very flat, which makes it ideal for plastic drainage. Plastic pipes have smoother bores than clay and can be laid flatter. Clay is usually laid at a gradient of one in forty; plastic can be laid as flat as one in two hundred.

That difference sounds minor until you translate it into digging and brickwork. With clay drainage, every forty-yard run means the sewer gets a yard deeper. Depth means manholes. Deep manholes mean brickwork, expense and disruption. With plastic laid at one in two hundred, the drain only drops a yard after two hundred yards. Shallow systems allow lower-cost plastic access chambers at junctions and changes of direction, with far less excavation.

In plain terms: it saves money — and contractors understand money even when they do not understand sales representatives.

Armed with my Marley training, I began taking contractors' contoured site drawings home and redesigning schemes: converting clay systems to plastic, showing the depth at each chamber and manhole. At first there was some resistance

The Export Adventurer

from Building Control — particularly in Selby — but it soon disintegrated. By 1980, I was the only representative from the Harrogate office earning a bonus.

There was another complication. Before the 1980s Marley had dealt directly with large construction companies and had made little effort to distribute through builders' merchants. This approach had upset many merchants, and you could be *persona non grata* in a surprising number of places.

I found the best way around that was simple: get the order from the contractor first, then take it to a builder's merchant and offer to put it through them as *their* order. This soothed bruised feelings, strengthened local supply, and let everyone look as though they had won.

Using orders I received from a very prominent housebuilder in York, we gained three stockists in the Mixconcrete Group.

I learned a lot at Marley. Technical competence mattered. Going the extra mile mattered. But the biggest lesson was this: people like to deal with friends. If possible, make friends with your clients.

Unfortunately, I also discovered a level of petty-mindedness — from the local office and from head office — that I found irritating after years of doing things my own way.

In 1981, because recession meant construction sites usually closed for Easter week, head office instructed all representatives to take Easter week off and deduct it from our holiday entitlement. I had already booked my holidays for the year. To comply, I would have had to cancel one of my planned holidays and lose the deposit.

The final straw came when Marley made one of the assistant sales managers redundant.

I decided enough was enough and began looking at the competition.

The merry-go-round

In the plastic pipes industry, sales representatives existed on a perpetual merry-go-round. We all met ex-colleagues at Interbuild and HVAC exhibitions at the NEC each year. One year you'd be with Marley, the next with Osma, then Key Terrain, and on to Bartol. Faces changed badges the way some people changed ties.

Bartol was looking for two representatives. I applied, along with the recently redundant Peter Woodhouse.

When I went to interview at Bartol with the UK Sales Director, Peter Marshall, and senior manager Len Wilkinson, it went well. During the interview, however, I was told there was also a vacancy for a senior manager in the Export Department. Would I be interested?

The export role was several pay grades higher than sales representative — though it came without a company car. I already owned a six-cylinder Volvo 164 for towing the caravan, so the lack of a vehicle did not trouble me. I decided to go for the export position.

Mr Marshall telephoned the export director, and I was whisked upstairs post-haste.

The export director, George Bell, was a gentle, kindly-looking man of about six foot two. He asked questions and probed my past. After half an hour he said, "I'll think about it overnight and let you know as soon as possible," adding that Peter Marshall was holding back on his own decision pending the outcome of my interview — meaning he would need to decide promptly.

I was escorted down to reception and had just left the front door, walking across to the visitors' car park, when a first-floor window opened and George's voice boomed across the forecourt:

"I've decided. When can you start?"

It was the Wednesday before Easter 1981. Before I could answer properly, I had to resign from Marley Extrusions.

I went home, wrote out my resignation letter, and first thing the following day drove up to Harrogate — fully prepared, if necessary, to come home by public transport.

Tom Allerdice, Marley's North-East Sales Manager, tried to persuade me to stay, but he could not get anywhere near the pay rise I was leaving for — an increase of around fifty percent. Marley required a month's notice and asked me to return the car at the end of that month.

Because I was joining a competitor, they did not want me visiting their customers during my notice period. I was given one month's gardening leave.

It was almost exactly a year since I had driven home in that lovely gleaming blue Cavalier on my first day.

George Bell was delighted when I phoned him to say I could come into the Bartol office even though Marley still technically employed me. On the Tuesday after Easter, I arrived and

The Export Adventurer

began settling in — aiming to become fully operational as quickly as possible.

It was the start of something new again.

If Marley had reminded me how large organisations really worked, Bartol was about to show me how export, politics and personality intersected on a far wider stage.

Chapter 7 — Bartol Plastics

I arrived at Bartol Plastics on Tuesday, 21 April 1981, driving my one-year-old Vauxhall Cavalier — still very much a Marley Extrusions company car. George Bell had been busy informing people of my imminent arrival, which caused something of a stir when it became known that I was still working my notice at Marley and still in possession of their vehicle.

I was shown to my office in the new office block. It was equipped with the latest telecommunications technology and located on the first floor overlooking Edlington Road and the main gate of the Yorkshire Main Colliery. It felt very different from my previous working environments — modern, purposeful, and slightly intimidating.

Although we were employed and paid by Bartol Plastics, the export department operated under the group banner of **Hepworth Plastics International Ltd**. Our responsibility at Doncaster was sales only. Invoicing, documentation, and payment collection were handled centrally by Hepworth Plastics' headquarters in Rugby.

The Hepworth group at that time consisted of Bartol Plastics in Doncaster; Hepworth Industrial Plastics in Burnley, manufacturing PVC pressure pipes; Fordham Plastics in Dudley, producing plastic baths and sinks; and Plastidrain, manufacturers of uPVC sewer systems, recently acquired and merged into Bartol.

George and I shared a secretary, Nicky, and we had six administration staff supporting the department. We were well equipped: electronic calculators, modern telephones, and other gadgets that would have seemed futuristic only a few years earlier. Nicky had just received a brand-new IBM "golf-ball" typewriter, which made a noise like a machine gun when she was in full flow.

Mid-morning and mid-afternoon, all senior managers and directors were invited to take coffee in the boardroom. These informal gatherings proved remarkably effective, allowing inter-departmental issues to be dealt with quickly and amicably, and saving endless memos and territorial wrangling.

For April 1981 I was paid by both Marley and Bartol. Because my P45 had not yet arrived, Bartol taxed me on the emergency code, which was painful but short-lived.

When Peter Marshall heard how quickly I had arrived — just days after he had interviewed me for a home-sales role — he came to my office to welcome me. He was particularly amused that although I was now with Bartol, I was still driving a Marley car and Marley was paying for the fuel. Rivalries between plastic plumbing manufacturers were healthy, and this small victory over the competition caused no end of quiet amusement.

Putting systems in place

One of the first things I did was introduce a system very similar to the one I had learned at the 'Copper Works': a structured approach to overseas markets, agents, and country information. Until then, staff relied heavily on Croner's *International Trade Guide* and personal memory.

At that time, Bartol's export business was concentrated in Saudi Arabia, the Emirates, Egypt, Kenya, and Nigeria. Reviewing the records, it was clear these markets had been developed opportunistically, usually following specific contracts rather than through deliberate market planning.

In Egypt, for example, the agent Nile Trading was also a major contractor. Their relationship with Bartol began when they needed British-standard plastic waste and sewer pipes for a new township project. In Saudi Arabia, the agent was BMTC-Wickes, an arrangement that arose through Bartol's home-sales relationship with the Wickes group in the UK.

Bartol supported its overseas partners well and had British expatriates stationed in Egypt, the Emirates, Kenya, and Nigeria. At the same time, many British contractors — Costain, Wimpey, Taylor Woodrow, McAlpine, Tarmac, and others — were operating internationally. Where they went, there was demand for British building products. By following the contractors, identifying new markets was often straightforward.

What was changing, however, was the backdrop.

As Britain's global influence declined and we aligned ourselves more closely with the European Economic Community, much of our historic Commonwealth trading network withered. We stopped buying New Zealand lamb and butter; they stopped buying from us. British Standards, once dominant across the Middle East, Africa, Australasia, the Caribbean, and parts of Asia, were gradually replaced by European standards agreed in Brussels. Markets that had once felt comfortably British were now shared with German, French, and Italian competitors.

New markets, new thinking

Malaysia developed almost effortlessly. In 1982, Plastics Centre (SDN) Berhad wrote to us asking if we would supply fittings while they extruded their own pipe. We had already done something similar in Nigeria, where Tate & Lyle extruded pipe locally and imported fittings from us.

George retained responsibility for East and South Africa and Spain — markets he had developed successfully — while I was given the title **Export Development Manager**. In the Bartol company magazine, George paraphrased *Star Trek*, describing me as "the man whose job was to go where no man had been before."

The nickname "Wicker" soon followed in the staff magazine, helped along by the number of unfamiliar countries I began visiting.

Around the same time, we were approached by a company trading throughout the Caribbean: Kings Worldwide. Their export business had grown from three furnishing shops in and around London, supplying hotels across the Leeward and Windward Islands with everything from bedding and carpets to plumbing, electrical, and fire-fighting equipment.

We had already supplied plumbing materials to some prestige Caribbean hotels through Kings. The owners — Albert and Lily Hammerson — and their son Charles combined holidays with marketing trips. Charles wanted to expand the business by broadening the product range and asked if I would accompany him on a short exploratory trip to assess the potential for setting up stockist distributors across the islands.

At the same time, one of the Chambers of Commerce was organising a trade mission to Trinidad. George and I decided it would be an excellent opportunity to investigate at relatively low cost.

Ireland and Europe

Another issue landed on our desks from home sales. Bartol had been supplying Ireland from a Belfast stock point, invoicing in sterling but being paid in Irish punts. Worse still, builders' merchants in the south owed Bartol £80,000.

George and I agreed that southern Ireland should be treated as an export market. On my first visit I collected £65,000 in cheques — some written in pencil — none of which bounced. I appointed a local agent to visit clients regularly, collect orders, and ensure prompt payment.

Meanwhile, Hepworth Industrial Plastics had acquired plastic double-glazing technology from Brugman Friesoplast in Germany, marketing the product in the UK as Hepworth Astraseal. Brugman's CEO, Ulf Brickenstein, had seen Bartol's Acorn push-fit plumbing system at Burnley and was keen to market it in Germany.

Interest also came from France, Belgium, Sweden, and the Netherlands, much of it sparked by contacts made at HVAC and Interbuild exhibitions at the NEC. Each exhibition alternated annually, and overseas visitors were plentiful.

How to find markets

Bartol needed new markets, and in our sector there were two proven ways to find them.

The Export Adventurer

The first was to follow projects from planning through to construction. Influence could be exerted at multiple levels: the project owner, the architect or consultant, the main contractor, or the plumbing and drainage subcontractor — depending on where quality, price, or ease of installation mattered most.

The second was to identify markets still using lead, copper, or cast-iron drainage systems, where British-standard plastic offered clear advantages and faced little resistance.

One of my early initiatives was to have an administrator read all the trade journals — *Construction News* and others — and extract details of projects with British influence, whether in design or construction. Iraq, Jordan, and Malaysia stood out. Iraq in particular was attractive: Saddam Hussein was rebuilding Baghdad in preparation for hosting the Non-Aligned Nations conference in 1986.

The challenge was that we had no export sales force roaming the globe to chase these opportunities.

The solution was obvious.

We would use the government's British Overseas Trade Board (BOTB) missions and exhibitions to explore these markets first-hand, learn quickly, and decide where to invest effort and money.

That decision opened the door to the most intense and far-reaching period of international travel in my career.

What followed was not occasional travel but sustained immersion — trade missions, frontier markets, and encounters that would test judgement, endurance, and sometimes nerve.

Chapter 8 — First Choice — The Preparation

The first market we chose to explore was Iraq.

The British Overseas Trade Board (BOTB) was sponsoring a British pavilion at the Baghdad International Fair, with space for around forty British exhibitors. I submitted our applications and was accepted for both funding and exhibition space. I recall being genuinely excited. Although I had already travelled to Jordan and Bahrain several times with BNA-Gowanbury, Baghdad conjured something far more exotic in my imagination.

A preparatory meeting was held in London with all the prospective exhibitors. We were taken through the do's and don'ts, the formalities, and the practical recommendations. The BOTB package was generous: return airfares for two people, exhibition booth space, accommodation, and subsistence were all included.

Freight was another matter. The appointed freight forwarders offered to consolidate exhibitors' material into forty-foot containers at very competitive rates per cubic metre. Shipping to Iraq at that time was far from straightforward. The port of Basra was closed, and the Iran–Iraq war was still raging.

The BOTB supplied standard exhibition booths of varying sizes within the pavilion, with larger external spaces available. I ordered a basic stand inside the pavilion and splurged on two chairs.

The next issue was endurance.

The Export Adventurer

The exhibition ran from eight in the morning until eight at night, seven days a week, for twenty-one days. On top of that, two or three days were required at the beginning to unpack and assemble the display, and at the end you were contractually obliged to clear everything away — adding another day or two. In the heat of Baghdad, working twelve-hour days for almost a month was going to be a formidable undertaking.

After discussion with George, we decided to ask Home Sales if they could loan us one of their sales representatives to help man the stand. I went to see Peter Marshall, half expecting resistance — after all, this meant depriving him of one of his people for a month.

Peter was entirely amenable. He saw it as an opportunity rather than a loss. A day or two later he came back to me with a suggestion: he proposed offering the Baghdad trip to one of his salesmen who happened to be the company's longest-serving employee. The man had joined Bartol in its infancy twenty years earlier and was due to retire in six months' time. Peter thought the trip would make a fitting thank-you gift.

A week later, the salesman — Eric Bolton — came to my office so we could discuss the trip and what would be expected of him. Toward the end of our meeting, Eric told me something that immediately reframed the whole exercise.

During the war he had served in the Guards Tank Regiment and had fought at El Alamein. He had always wanted to return and visit the battlefield and had already studied maps, but Baghdad was a long way from Cairo and El Alamein, and he assumed it would not be possible to combine the two.

He went on to describe how after El Alamein his regiment had fought in the Italian campaign at Monte Cassino, before being withdrawn prior to Anzio and shipped back to the UK. From

The Export Adventurer

there, they took part in the Normandy landings. Despite all this history, he confirmed he was keen and genuinely looking forward to Baghdad.

At Bartol and Hepworth we always travelled on full-fare air tickets, precisely because they allowed changes to schedules — which were almost inevitable. I rang our travel agent and asked what the additional cost would be if Eric routed home via Cairo.

There was none.

We also had two Bartol sales personnel based in Cairo, both living on Zamalek, the island in the Nile at the centre of the city. I sent them a telex — this was still the pre-fax, pre-email era — explaining the situation and asking whether either of them could put Eric up for a couple of nights and take him out to El Alamein on one of his free days.

The reply from Phil and Simon was immediate and enthusiastic. They would be delighted.

I ran the idea past George and Peter, who both thought it a wonderful gesture. The arrangements were authorised, as the entire exercise could be done at effectively zero cost, apart from a day or two's subsistence.

We decided to keep it a surprise.

I gave Eric only the outbound flight from Heathrow and the return date and time. Nicky typed up his full itinerary — flights, hotels, contact numbers — including accommodation details in Cairo. When I handed him the tickets a few days before departure, he leafed through them, stopped, and stared.

Tears welled up in his eyes.

The Export Adventurer

"I'm going to Cairo," he said quietly.

With the preparations complete, and expectations running high, it was time to discover whether reality in Baghdad would match imagination.

Chapter 9 — Baghdad Fair

I flew to Baghdad in late September 1981, a few days ahead of Eric. Somewhat unexpectedly, a technical representative from our sister company, Hepworth Industrial Plastics, Alistair Pollard, joined me at the last moment.

Alistair was well over six feet tall, so when we checked in for the direct Iraqi Airways flight, he requested extra legroom. We were allocated seats directly in front of a door. These are acceptable until people start wandering about, peering through the door window and tripping over your feet. There is also nowhere to put a gin and tonic without effectively sealing yourself in behind the tray table. Still, it was only a four-hour flight.

Alistair was pursuing a major water-distribution project for the city of Kerbala, about seventy kilometres south of Baghdad. Our Egyptian agent, Nile Trading, already had the contract; Alistair's role was to dot the i's and cross the t's with the Ministry and consulting engineers. He also intended to visit another project in Dohuk, in the extreme north of Iraq.

After flying over Jordan, as we approached the Iraqi border the cabin crew announced that all window blinds had to be closed — an unusual instruction at thirty thousand feet in broad daylight. Aircraft doors, however, do not have blinds. When I looked out, I saw we were being escorted from the border by two Russian-built Iraqi MiG fighters, one on each wing.

The Foreign Office had assured us that despite the Iran–Iraq war still raging, Baghdad was safe to visit. I remember thinking that perhaps someone had forgotten to tell the Iraqis.

The Export Adventurer

We landed at the old airport, which served both civilian and military traffic. As we taxied in, we passed rows of MiG fighters parked beneath concrete blast shelters, with camouflaged transporters tucked away around the perimeter. Immigration and security were thorough — every bag and suitcase was opened and searched.

Further doubts about safety arose as we drove into central Baghdad. Barrage balloons still floated above key communications buildings and the main post office. Almost every building — schools and hospitals included — had steel rooftop water tanks painted in camouflage, giving the city an oddly militarised appearance.

We attended a briefing at the British Embassy, where the ambassador went through a list of do's and don'ts and issued our exhibition passes. One instruction was to avoid ice in drinks, as it was made from tap water stored in rooftop tanks that were often open to the elements and ideal breeding grounds for mosquitoes.

I remain convinced that if you are going to catch a water-borne bug, it will be from the glass washed in it or the salad rinsed in it. And so it proved: everyone eventually succumbed to what became universally known as *Baghdad belly*.

At the exhibition site in the Mansour district, we were relieved to find that our exhibits had already been delivered to the British Pavilion. Our marketing department had done a superb job: all displays were mounted on six-by-four-foot boards. We simply stood them up and screwed them into place. We were finished in no time.

The heat, however, was relentless. Soft drinks were served at room temperature, cooled only by the very ice we had been

The Export Adventurer

warned against. A warm, sugary drink in intense heat is remarkably ineffective at quenching thirst.

A few days later, Alan Nelson, export manager at Hepworth Industrial Plastics, arrived to join Alistair on trips to Kerbala and Dohuk. Alan had been to Baghdad before, although his navigation depended entirely on returning to his original hotel on Abu Nuwas and starting again from there.

Because of their planned travel north and south, we hired a car. On collecting it, we noticed a hefty per-kilometre surcharge. Given the distances involved, Alistair and Alan decided to disconnect the speedometer cable. We failed to reach it behind the dashboard but succeeded at the gearbox.

When Eric arrived, Alistair and Alan departed for Dohuk. That region, near Mosul, was volatile: Kurdish unrest was ongoing, and they were required to hire an armed escort to proceed beyond Mosul. They returned two days later with stories of roadblocks and tension — and a car interior coated in an eighth of an inch of fine beige dust.

Mazgouf by the River Tigris

While they were away, Eric and I ran the stand. I discovered a Baghdad speciality called *masgouf* — carp caught live from the Tigris, killed, split, and slow-barbecued over open fires along the riverbank. We selected our fish on Abu Nuwas, paid around £30, and carried it into a nearby restaurant that provided the mezza, bread, and beer.

The flesh was so delicate it fell from the bones. We were advised to use split pitta bread as fingers, which worked perfectly.

The exhibition itself divided neatly into two halves. Mornings were for trade and government visitors; afternoons were open to the public. To my amazement, everyone on our target list eventually visited our stand: the State Organisation for Housing Implementation, Baghdad Sewerage Board, the Ministry for Roads, along with numerous contractors, architects, and consultants. Many construction firms were foreign — Indian, South Korean, French, German, and British.

Afternoons were long, hot, and punctuated by waves of schoolchildren hunting promotional giveaways. I had brought five hundred Hepworth cotton beanie hats and amused myself by handing one or two to children on neighbouring stands, triggering stampedes before strolling away.

Food shortages were obvious. Beef, lamb, and goat went to the army. Pork was out of the question. That left chicken — every conceivable variety, provided it was chicken. One weary exhibitor asked for an omelette and was told solemnly, "All chickens dead."

The Export Adventurer

Ali Baba round about

At the Petra Hotel one evening, I was startled to see an old colleague from the Copper Works dining nearby. It reminded me just how small the world can be.

When Eric left for Cairo, Alistair and I took him to the airport. He was buzzing with excitement. On returning to the hotel, I found a telex from George Bell:

Sadat assassinated. Under no circumstances is Eric Bolton to travel to Cairo.

I had no choice but to reply that Eric was already airborne.

President Anwar Sadat had been assassinated in Cairo that very day, 6 October 1981, during a military parade. The Middle East reacted instantly. That evening, Iraqi troops fired tracer rounds into the air in celebration. Four people were reportedly killed when the bullets fell back to earth.

Fortunately, our colleagues in Cairo intercepted Eric at the airport. He reached El Alamein the following day without incident.

During the fair we met many people with whom we would build long-term relationships. One was Tariq Shaikley, already established in mechanical services. When we decided it would

The Export Adventurer

cost more to repatriate our exhibits than they were worth, Tariq asked for them as samples.

We attempted to remove them — unsuccessfully. Armed guards decided otherwise and dumped all the plastic fittings into a skip, though they spared the literature. After a thorough dressing-down, we were released.

On our final evening someone reversed into our hire car, crushing the front wing. When reconnecting the speedometer we discovered the inner cable missing. Tariq arranged a local repair, but it still cost £400 — an expensive reminder that in Iraq, annoying the authorities when you require an exit visa is unwise.

With the Fair concluded — and lessons learned at every level — the next stage would take us further afield, testing both stamina and judgement in ways no exhibition ever could.

Chapter 10 — The Baghdad Sewerage Board

On my next visit to Baghdad following the Fair, I called at the offices of John Haiste & Partners, the consulting engineers to the Baghdad Sewerage Board.

They explained that the Board had developed a serious problem and required a specialised trap for road gullies.

Over many years, thousands of concrete road gullies had been installed throughout the city to drain surface water. Each gully discharged into a 250 mm outside-diameter PVC pipe set into the side wall. Originally, this design worked perfectly well because the drainage system discharged directly into the River Tigris.

However, with the introduction of a new foul sewer system across the city, it became unavoidable to combine surface water and foul drainage. This allowed odorous sewer gases to flow back up the system and vent directly through the road gullies — not something the population of Baghdad appreciated.

The Sewerage Board therefore needed a trap that could be fitted into the internal bore of the 250 mm PVC outlet pipe to prevent foul gases escaping into the gully. The trap had to be a simple hand-push fit and easily removable, allowing periodic cleaning of the gully.

This was far from straightforward.

Plastic pipes, regardless of the standard to which they are made, are extruded with very tight tolerances on the outside diameter to ensure correct fit into fittings. However, there are fewer constraints on wall thickness, meaning that the internal diameter (bore) can vary significantly — especially when pipes come from multiple manufacturers.

In Baghdad, this variability was compounded by the fact that several different manufacturers had supplied the original pipes. The consultants explained that Greek manufacturers had already declined to quote for such a trap, believing it impossible to guarantee a reliable water- and air-tight seal over such a variable bore.

Nor did such a product exist in anyone's catalogue.

Just one week before travelling to Baghdad, I had been finishing the installation of a bathroom in an extension at my own house. As the consultants spoke, the solution suddenly sprang to mind.

The multi-quick WC pan connector.

This humble fitting solves almost exactly the same problem. It seals onto the outside of ceramic WC outlet spigots — which also vary in diameter — using a series of flexible rubber fins to form a water- and air-tight seal.

Armed with nothing more than a sketch of the concept — the consultants had no technical drawings — and the principle of flexible fins firmly in mind, I took the enquiry back to Bartol–Hepworth.

The initial reaction was predictable.

"Why don't you sell what we already make?"

The Export Adventurer

However, once production and finance realised that the Sewerage Board wanted 50,000 units, attitudes changed rapidly. We worked with our technical team and designed the trap together.

Once the design was finalised, we ordered prototype EPDM synthetic rubber seals and had the body manufactured by a specialist plastic-welding company in Rotherham. The prototype was then passed to production to estimate tooling and production costs.

Robin Platt, the Finance Director, eventually told me that if I could achieve £4.00 per unit ex works, he would be more than satisfied.

The Board, however, wanted the traps delivered to their warehouse in Baghdad.

Basra, Iraq's only seaport, remained closed due to the Iran–Iraq war, so shipment had to go via Aleppo in Syria and then overland to Baghdad. This increased the delivered cost to £4.20 per unit.

On my next visit to Baghdad, I took the prototype with me. The Director-General of the Baghdad Sewerage Board, Mr Farid Shamir, arranged for a team of his engineers, representatives of John Haiste & Partners, and engineers from the six Indian and Korean contracting companies involved to escort me around the city.

For several days we tested the prototype in gullies at numerous locations. Each organisation arrived in its own Jeep, Land Cruiser, or Range Rover.

The Export Adventurer

At one point, a contractor's senior engineer remarked that my convoy was four vehicles longer than Saddam Hussein's, who had passed along the same road earlier that day.

The prototype worked perfectly in every location.

We returned to the Sewerage Board for an audience with the Director-General. He sat in a vast room furnished with ten or so four-seater settees, all occupied by people patiently awaiting his attention.

We joined them, drank several cups of tea, and waited.

Eventually, Mr Shamir spoke in Arabic to one of his engineers who had been with us during the site trials. I understood very little. He then spoke to the British consultant — from Leeds — and the conversation switched to English. Finally, he turned to me.

"Mr Bratley," he asked, "how much are your traps?"

"Four point two," I replied.

He raised his hand, cutting me off before I could add *pounds sterling*, and spoke briefly to his engineer again.

Then he turned back to me.

"Four dinar twenty is within our budget. Please go with Miss Zuhail to Accounts. They will prepare the letter of credit."

I thanked him and followed Miss Zuhail out of the room.

Four dinars twenty was £9.80.

The Export Adventurer

On an order of 50,000 units, we had just secured a contract worth nearly £500,000 and cleared over £280,000 more profit than had been built into the original costing.

Within an hour, Miss Zuhail handed me a copy of the letter of credit for £490,000, drawn on Rafidain Bank and confirmed in London.

That evening, I invited the two engineers from John Haiste & Partners and their wives out to celebrate. We went to the best restaurant in Baghdad — the National Restaurant at the Al-Rashid Hotel.

One engineer's wife was Italian. Scanning the menu, she exclaimed,
"Oh look, John — they have Dom Pérignon."

I assured her she was free to order whatever she wished.

She ordered a bottle at 45 dinars (£90) — and then another.

With dinner for five, the bill came to £740 (1984 prices).

A day or two later, I was bumped off a direct Iraqi Airways flight to London due to a reservations mix-up. Rather than lose another day rerouting through Amman, I upgraded to first class at a cost of £400.

When I arrived back in Doncaster, I went straight into George Bell's office.

"I've got some good news and some bad news," I said.

George replied, "I've had a torrid time while you've been away. Give me the good news first."

The Export Adventurer

I told him we had secured the Baghdad Sewerage Board order.

He was delighted.

Then I told him the unit price — and the extra profit.

George jumped up and hugged me.

"So what's the bad news?" he asked.

"It took a £740 dinner to get the order," I said, "and £400 to get it home."

George responded succinctly:
"F*** that."

Two further major orders followed almost immediately — for the Al-Sadia and Zafrania new townships — seemingly from nowhere. In fact, they traced directly back to contacts made at the Baghdad Fair.

The State Organisation for Housing Implementation had approached me there for an urgent quotation. Using my Marley training, I extracted quantities directly from drawings and specifications and priced the work in Baghdad.

We won the orders on one condition.

They wanted an engineer on site for three months to teach them how to install plastic systems.

They had only ever used cast iron.

Supplying materials was one thing. Teaching an entire

workforce to abandon generations of habit was something else entirely — and it would take me deeper into Iraq than any trade fair ever could.

Chapter 11 — The Iraq Market

Saddam Hussein had bid for — and been awarded — the honour of hosting the 1986 Non-Aligned Conference. Iraq intended to show the world how far it had advanced, and Baghdad was being rebuilt with that single aim in mind. New bridges sprang up across the Tigris. New hotels rose almost as quickly as the cranes could move: the Novotel, the Ishtar Sheraton, the Palestine Meridian along the strip between Sadoun Street and Abu Nuwas, and the Al Rashid just across from the giant crossed-swords parade ground.

By then I had already enjoyed early success in Iraq: the Baghdad Sewerage Board trap and two new township contracts. Our sister company, Hepworth Industrial Plastics, was doing well too, with projects in Kerbala and the development of Tagit Island. Over the next two or three years, colleagues joined me on trips, and as our business expanded, our accommodation improved in step — culminating in the almost absurd luxury of the Al Rashid.

Al Rashid Hotel Baghdad

Baghdad itself, and the surrounding region, offered a concentration of history that felt bottomless. In and around the city there were ancient wonders: the Khadamire Mosque, Tagit Island, the Copper Souk. A short distance away lay Kerbala and Babylon. Beyond that, Iraq was a catalogue of places that had lived in books long before they appeared on a hotel itinerary: Erbil, the Ziggurat of Ur, Hatra, Dur-Kurigalzu, Sulaymaniyah, Ctesiphon, Mosul, Nineveh, and the Zakho mosque, to name only a few.

BABYLON (Remains of the walls)

Between trips and work, I — sometimes with Alistair Pollard, sometimes with Brian Wallington or Simon Murray — managed to get out to Tagit Island, Kerbala, the Ishtar Gate and Babylon. Before the Iran–Iraq war, Iraq had even developed tourist facilities that sounded improbable for a desert nation: ski resorts in the northern mountains near the Turkish border.

Yet beneath all the building, the atmosphere was unmistakably controlled. Every shop, office, hotel and public building displayed a mandatory photograph of Saddam Hussein. Iraqis would not enter into any conversation where government — and certainly Saddam — was the subject. Many disliked the dictatorship, but they were afraid of being overheard. Tariq would sometimes make disparaging comments in his car, then warn us that everywhere — particularly hotels — was bugged.

At first I took that with a pinch of salt. Then one night in the Al Rashid, an extraordinarily bright red LED on the television caught my eye when I was trying to sleep. I turned the TV off, but the LED stayed lit. I unplugged the set completely.

I fell asleep.

A knock at the door woke me. A hotel maintenance man informed me there was "something wrong with my TV", checked it, and plugged it back in.

From that point onward, I took Tariq's warnings rather more seriously.

Brian Wallington, Simon Murray and me inside the Palestine Meridian (note the concrete spiders web on the balcony)

The Palestine Meridian later became the UN headquarters during the occupation after Desert Storm. Its exterior has a distinctive concrete spider-web shading over each balcony. In photographs I took before the UN moved in, you can see right through those concrete webs into the rooms behind the patio doors. History has a habit of leaving fingerprints on buildings.

The Palestine Meridien was used by the NATO forces as its HQ and it was attacked several times.

Watching the company from afar

Back home, Hepworth was going through a cost-cutting exercise. The plan was to merge sales and administration functions across Bartol–Hepworth and Hepworth Industrial Plastics. Price Waterhouse was mapping tasks and analysing who did what. I suspected that at least one export manager would be made redundant.

As it turned out, most of the consolidation hit administration rather than sales. The product ranges were so different that major changes in home or export selling simply did not make sense.

Alan Nelson: time, nerves, and "Engineer Akmed"

Alan Nelson was a good man: dedicated, hardworking, and willing to graft for long hours. He also became, unintentionally, one of the more entertaining travelling companions I ever had.

In front of clients, he could be slightly nervous. He had a habit of opening his briefcase and almost hiding behind the lid, as though it were a portable blast shield. But he was persistent. When we were in Baghdad, we were forever calling at Nile Trading. Alan repeatedly asked to see Engineer Akmed, and every time we called, Engineer Akmed was "out of the office". This went on daily for more than a week.

Alan also had one weakness that affected everyone within a five-mile radius: timekeeping. If you wanted to leave the hotel at eight, you had to tell Alan it was seven, otherwise you would spend your life waiting in lobbies.

On one occasion we had secured a dinner reservation at a popular restaurant near the Petra Hotel. Getting a booking there was no mean feat. I arrived promptly. Our guests were already seated. Alan was nowhere to be seen. Ten minutes passed. Fifteen. Twenty. The maître d' grew visibly anxious.

I rang the hotel and asked for Alan's room.

When he answered, I adopted my best Middle Eastern accent and told him that if he did not arrive within ten minutes, the reservation would be cancelled.

Five minutes later Alan came flying through the restaurant doors with shaving foam still around his ears. I thanked him — still in the same accent.

The following day I called at his room on my way to mine. The door was ajar and I could hear him speaking, so I knocked and walked in.

He was on the telephone, saying, "I know who it is."

He turned, saw me, and went completely white. Then, in a suddenly much more respectful tone, he said, "Yes, Engineer Akmed… it's so nice to hear from you."

Breakfast, logistics, and tea in a coffee cup

On another morning, we were due to travel out into the desert. I waited for Alan in the hotel restaurant. At that early hour the place was empty except for me. By the time he arrived, I had already eaten boiled eggs, toast and coffee and was about to leave.

The Export Adventurer

Most of the restaurant staff were Egyptian, brought in to replace Iraqis who had been drafted into the army. One waiter circulated with a jug of tea, very hot water and a tin of Nescafé. He had been trained to follow a set route around the room, so even if there was only one occupied table in the whole restaurant, you still had to wait until the route brought him past you before you could get a drink.

Alan, desperate to catch up, did not have time for the route. When the waiter finally reached us, Alan grabbed the tin of Nescafé, spooned granules into his cup, snatched the jug from the tray and poured tea straight over the coffee.

It was not, in strict terms, what anyone would call breakfast. But it was certainly efficient.

"Cook, he has no watch"

We were often joined at breakfast by other exhibitors. One was Dick Lovett, a Midlands manufacturer of standby generators. Dick had a precise breakfast requirement: two eggs boiled for four minutes.

Some days his eggs arrived raw. Other days they arrived rock hard, with yolks turning black. Each morning he became more emphatic, using his fingers to illustrate the order: "Two eggs" (two fingers), "four minutes" (four fingers). After a week, Dick finally asked the waiter why, after repeated instructions, the eggs were sometimes raw and sometimes overcooked.

The waiter looked at him for a long time — so long it felt deliberate — and then replied:

"Cook… he has no watch."

The Export Adventurer

George in Baghdad

As our sales grew in Iraq, my boss, George Bell, decided he wanted to see the market for himself.

We flew to Amman, where we had a choice of two air-shuttle services into Baghdad: Royal Jordanian or Iraqi Airways. During the Iran–Iraq conflict, they were the only carriers still servicing the route. Both were using Boeing 747 jumbo jets for a one-hour flight — an extraordinary machine to deploy for what was, in effect, an 800-kilometre desert drive that nobody in their right mind wanted to attempt.

We overnighted at the Amman Intercontinental. The next morning, at Queen Alia Airport, we discovered we had been bumped off the flight — common at the time.

A melee of disgruntled passengers had formed around the check-in desk, all trying to get the clerk's attention. To be reinstated, you had to reach the front and explain that you had not broken your journey for more than twenty-four hours. Under international airline rules, that meant you were still classed as "in transit", and they were obliged to honour your booking.

George charged straight into the scrum.

I stayed back with the cases and watched the chaos. Then the gold braid caught my eye: a very senior member of the airline staff emerged from an office and walked behind the check-in desks. I leapt over an empty check-in counter, intercepted him, and apologised for vaulting the furniture. I explained our situation calmly: we were still within transit limits, and we needed reinstating.

He agreed instantly, returned to his office, and reappeared moments later with two boarding passes. He checked our baggage in at the vacant desk as though the whole business had been planned.

Boarding passes in hand, I turned to rescue George — just as he spotted the same officer walking back to his office. George sprang onto the baggage scales to get behind the desks at the precise moment the clerk pressed the conveyor button.

George's legs were taken clean from under him. He disappeared onto the floor behind the counters in a puff of dust and airport archaeology: cigarette ends and empty cockroach shells.

He struggled upright and retreated towards me, brushing detritus from his clothes with dignity that was only partial.

"I nearly got him," he said, with resignation.

The Dar es Salaam

In Baghdad we checked into our hotel: the Dar es Salaam on Sadoun Street.

Accommodation was so scarce that sharing a room was standard. I always found it more acceptable when you shared with someone you already knew. The room had a functional en-suite, but it had clearly been designed for one person. With the extra bed squeezed in, you had to stand on my bed to open the wardrobe and stand on George's bed to open the balcony doors.

The hotel was infested with miniature cockroaches.

That first evening, George and I sat up in bed drinking Johnnie Walker whisky — partly in defiance of local cuisine, partly to "neutralise any bugs" — and smoking King Edward cigars, blowing the smoke at the walls in the hopeful belief it might discourage the wildlife.

The following day there was a knock at the door. The housemaid asked whether she could make up the room.

George invited her in and whispered to me, "I'll show you how to get good service in a hotel."

He took a ten-dinar note from his wallet, held it out and said, "This is for you. And if you look after us well, there will be another one when we leave."

The maid was thrilled.

We went down for breakfast.

We never saw her again.

I suggested to George that he may have just financed her fare home.

The seminar, the projector, and the embassy dash

George had insisted on bringing a company 35mm film to Iraq. The plan was to arrange a presentation — at the British Embassy, the British Council, or hotel facilities — and draw in as many officials and contractors as possible. To do it, we needed a projector we could rent or borrow.

We were told that Mrs Pauletti at the British Embassy had one.

So, we made an appointment.

Taxis in Baghdad were tricky. Most able-bodied Iraqi men between 18 and 45 were in the army; drivers tended to be older, infirm, or foreign. During my early trips I had also become convinced that some taxi drivers were security services. Despite the shortage, I often found the same driver waiting whenever I left the hotel.

On this occasion we secured a taxi for the half-hour journey to the embassy in Al Mansour. Partway there, George realised — too late — that something he'd eaten was reacting against him.

The embassy sat in extensive grounds, with a drive 200 to 300 yards long. For security, no vehicles were allowed past the Gurkha guards at the gate, so visitors had to walk the full length.

George's strides became shorter and shorter. Seeing his distress, I offered to walk ahead and find the toilets.

At the reception window, two or three people were already queuing. George was still well behind me. I waited my turn and just as I reached the front and began explaining who we were, a large hairy arm barged me sideways.

George gasped, "Where's the bog?"

The Sheriff

On another occasion, George's partially bald head had burned in the desert sun. In the taxi back to the hotel he asked me to drop him on Al Razak Street so he could buy a hat.

Twenty minutes later I reached the hotel. George arrived shortly afterwards with a brown paper bag which he placed in the wardrobe.

The next morning we rose at 6 a.m. and took a pre-booked taxi out into the desert to a French Kier site, where they were installing our mains water pressure pipes. It was early, the sun was still low, and George left the hat in the taxi.

By 10 a.m. the sun was brutal. I pointed out the fierce sunlight beating down on his still unprotected head.

George replied, "If I put my hat on, you've got to promise you won't laugh."

"Why would I laugh?" I asked.

"Just don't," he said.

He retrieved the brown paper bag, removed the hat, put it on, and looked at me as I tried — and failed — to stifle a belly laugh.

A large silver star with the word **SHERRIF** was emblazoned across the front.

He offered, hopefully, "Arabs don't wear hats, do they?"

The best plastics man I ever met

George was technically the most competent person I ever encountered in plastics. He had started as technical manager at Bartol. When export enquiries began coming in, orders needed someone who could advise customers on design and installation, and George was the only person capable of doing that. He grew into export from pure technical necessity.

At first, he knew little about international trade, but he learned quickly. By the time I joined his team, he was a highly competent exporter.

He was also the best manager I ever worked for. He knew his limitations and surrounded himself with people whose experience complemented his own.

One day, out on the plains of Babylon, the chief engineer for French Kier was short of a single 6" × 4" reducing fitting. Without it, their project would be delayed a week while a replacement was flown out from the UK.

George looked at the engineer and said, "If you can give me two feet of four-inch pipe, I'll make one by tomorrow."

The engineer was ecstatic and produced a length of pipe. I privately thought George had promised the impossible.

We went straight back into Baghdad and into Tariq Shaikley's office. George asked Tariq if he knew a woodworking shop with a lathe capable of turning timber to seven inches diameter.

We found one. George produced a technical drawing on the spot. Half an hour later we walked out with a wooden tapered former.

Next we called at a motor factor and bought five gallons of radiator antifreeze.

Back at Tariq's warehouse, a gas burner was set up and the antifreeze boiled in a galvanised bucket. After about half an hour George told me to put the pipe in. The pipe was too long to stand upright by itself; it would topple, taking the bucket and boiling liquid with it.

So I stood as far back as I could from the sweet-smelling cauldron and held the pipe steady with one finger.

When the PVC softened, it buckled under its own weight. The bucket tipped off the burner. The boiling antifreeze hit the cold damp floor, and a huge cloud of vapour erupted, temporarily blinding everyone.

George shouted, "Gerry!"

I didn't answer. I still had the softened pipe in my hand and the wooden former at my feet. In the confusion I pushed the pipe down onto the plug and knocked it into position, expanding one end from four inches to six.

When the vapour cleared, George peered through the haze. Seeing I was still standing, he said, with great feeling, "Thank goodness you're alright. I thought you'd been boiled alive."

I had been very fortunate. I'd been leaning forward, and my trousers hung loosely away from my legs, so although the front of my grey suit was speckled with black spots, I wasn't burned.

We had our improvised reducer. French Kier completed the connection and the job continued without delay.

George told me to buy a new suit and put it on expenses. When I got home the stains disappeared completely after dry cleaning — though I still took him up on the new suit.

Beige dust and cornflake engineering

Wherever you walk between the Tigris and Euphrates — the plains of Babylon, including Baghdad — the soil is an extremely fine beige alluvial dust that blows constantly in clouds. It is as fine as a new bag of cement. When you walk through it, it ripples away from your feet like water. It gets into everything: cars, machinery, and every stitch hole in your shoes.

George always wore Hush Puppies, still with crepe soles in those days. Because taxis were scarce, we walked whenever we could — four or five miles daily. It was a twenty-minute walk from our hotel to Sinak Square where Tariq's office was, and we often walked there and back at least once a day. The Sewerage Board, John Haiste & Partners, and Nile Trading were all within a mile of the hotel.

All that walking eventually put a hole clean through George's crepe soles.

One evening I returned to the room to find him with a large pair of scissors, cutting shoe inserts from a Cornflakes packet like a man preparing for war with breakfast cereal.

The wedding and the pressing problem

During that visit we were invited to the wedding of Tariq Shaikley's sister.

The Export Adventurer

Tariq on the ferry to Tajit Island in the Tigris

I unpacked a new tailor-made suit and a shirt I had made in Hong Kong, still in the tailor's plastic carrier. George, as usual, had packed at the last minute and crushed everything into his suitcase.

He took one look at my pristine suit, then at his own horizontally pleated version, and said in his Derbyshire twang, "I can't go with thee looking like that."

He rang the laundry and asked for his suit to be pressed.

Five minutes later a laundry boy arrived carrying a plastic bag full of oddments and emptied them onto the bed. He thought George had lost something. George held up his suit and mimed ironing.

The boy rang the laundry. The conversation was Arabic, with occasional English words — "iron", "electric" — so we knew he had the message. He put the phone down and said, "I am sorry, sir… he has no steam."

George replied, "Tell him not to worry about steam. An electric iron will do. This isn't a new suit. I just want the creases flattening."

The boy rang again. More Arabic. He put the phone down.

"I am sorry, sir… he is tired."

George's face darkened.

"You tell the idle bastard that if he doesn't press my suit in five minutes, I'm going to have his guts for garters!"

The boy rang again. This time the boy smiled — he'd been given a solution. He put the receiver down and announced, helpfully:

"Sir, we can press your suit in two minutes… tomorrow."

Shoes, sun, and dignity

I brought out my polished tan brogues. George stared at them and asked how I had got them so clean. I told him I had washed them.

He disappeared into the bathroom and returned holding dripping wet Hush Puppies and asked how I got mine dry.

I said, "I washed them four days ago and left them behind the basin pedestal to dry slowly."

Realising he had no time, George stood on the bed, opened the balcony doors and placed his shoes in full sun.

When he retrieved them just before we left, they had dried so quickly they had curled up, toe almost touching heel. He had to wet them again to get them back onto his feet.

The wedding reception was only a short walk from our hotel, between Sadoun Street and Nidal Street. George made a negative into a positive.

The Export Adventurer

"My feet are lovely and cool on this hot pavement," he said.

He didn't realise he was leaving wet footprints that clearly showed the hole in his sole.

In fairness, in Baghdad's dry heat the creases dropped out of George's suit as we walked. By the time we reached the hall his suit and shoes looked more than passable.

The Iraqi wedding

Inside, the reception had double doors into an anteroom, then another set of double doors into the hall itself. George and I were seated on a low settee positioned perfectly in line with the entrances. Everyone had to pass us.

We did nothing but stand up, smile, shake hands and sit down again for two hours.

We were the prize exhibits.

I noticed George's shoes were drying into whitish-grey tide marks. I asked him whether he'd brought his hat.

"Why?" he asked. "Do you like it now?"

"No," I said, "but you could have put it over your shoes."

Smelling the potential

On another occasion we were in the northern suburbs, Al A'Zamiyah — laid out in a modern grid of roads lined with white-painted villas. Wastewater and foul sewerage ran in open ditches alongside the streets, black-green with decomposing waste, methane bubbling to the surface.

George sniffed and said, "It's the only place in the world where I can literally smell the potential."

That reminds me of a conversation on a flight home. A fellow passenger asked my line of business.

"Plastic pipes for soil, waste, drainage and sewers," I said.

He replied, "Oh, what a terrible way to make a living."

I was irritated and probably shouldn't have answered, but I did:

"Look mate, it might be excrement to you, but it's my bread and butter."

Flies, ice, and other Baghdad realities

One day George asked me to look over the balcony at the back of the hotel. A chef was butchering meat in a small yard behind the kitchens. George pointed to a knife lying on a low wall with a blade that looked black.

I was about to ask what was unusual when the chef picked it up and the blade turned silver as the flies lifted off.

The Export Adventurer

Another day we were travelling along Sadoun Street when a huge block of ice — about two feet by two feet by six feet — slid off a utility vehicle and smashed into the taxi behind us. The taxi was a write-off. By the time the police arrived, the ice had melted away.

I know I've gone on a bit with the funnies — many of them involving George. I want to make it clear: George was far more than a boss to me. He was a very good friend. If he had ever written his own book, I'm sure there would have been many laughs at my expense.

"Why do you want to buy a parachute?"

Al Razak Street was a long street full of shoe shops. One evening, when I was in Baghdad alone, I decided to wander and see whether there were any bargains.

I hailed a taxi and instructed the driver to take me to Al Razak Street.

He asked what I wanted.

I assumed he was asking where along the street I wanted to be dropped, so I told him I wanted to buy a pair of shoes.

He looked at me quizzically, drove on, and when we reached the shoe shops he turned and asked:

"Why do you want to buy a parachute?"

The Export Adventurer

Teaching Cast Iron Men to Trust Plastic

The most important thing I learned in Iraq was that you can win a contract on price, but you only keep it on confidence.

The State Organisation for Housing Implementation gave us two substantial township orders — Al-Sadia and Zafrania — on one condition. They wanted an engineer on site for three months to advise on installation.

They had used cast iron for years. Plastic, to them, was not a product. It was a rumour.

From their point of view, the objections were entirely reasonable. Cast iron was heavy, rigid and reassuring. If you dropped it on your foot it broke bones, which only strengthened the impression that it was "proper". Plastic was light, flexible and suspiciously easy to cut. Anything that simple could not possibly last.

And there was another problem: the local workforce had learned its habits on cast iron. Those habits were not transferable.

With cast iron, you could be a little rough. With plastic, you had to be accurate. You had to cut square, deburr, allow for movement, understand sockets, tolerances, seals, fall, venting and access points. Most of all, you had to understand that plastic does not forgive improvisation. It simply leaks — often later, and usually in a place that guarantees maximum embarrassment.

So we supplied the engineer.

The first week was always the same. The site teams were polite, sceptical and determined to show that they didn't need

The Export Adventurer

instruction. They would listen to the explanation, nod gravely, and then do it the way they had always done it. The result was a collection of beautiful new plastic systems installed with cast-iron thinking.

That was when the real teaching began.

The method was not lectures. Lectures make enemies. The method was simple demonstrations and very small humiliations. You let them do it their way, then you tested it. When it failed, you did not say "I told you so". You just smiled, handed them the correct tool, and said, "Try it like this."

Once they saw the seals work — properly lubricated, properly aligned, properly inserted — something shifted. Plastic began to feel less like a gamble and more like a system.

It helped that Iraq provided constant practical examples of what happened when foul drainage was treated casually. In parts of Baghdad, foul water ran openly in roadside channels, black-green with methane bubbling to the surface. The smell alone was an argument for doing the work properly. Even George, who could find a joke in anything, once sniffed the air and said it was the only place he had ever been where he could literally smell the potential.

The next step was confidence in the fittings.

The men wanted to see strength. So the engineer would pick up a length of pipe and show that it could flex without cracking. He would show the difference between a clean cut and a hacked one. He would demonstrate deburring, then show how the same joint, badly finished, could ruin a seal. He would show why fall mattered, why rodding access mattered, and why a system that "seemed fine" today could become a nightmare six months later.

The Export Adventurer

Within a month, the tone changed. They began to call the engineer over before they assembled the awkward bits, not after. The questions became practical rather than defensive. And once the foremen started trusting it, the rest followed.

By the time the three months were nearly up, the cast-iron men were not only installing plastic — they were explaining it to others, with the confidence of people who had always known.

Which is how you know you've won.

Not when they stop arguing.

When they start teaching.

Last Trip to Iraq

On my final trip to Baghdad, I met up with Simon Murray, who had moved from Cairo and taken up residence in Amman. Amman proved to be a far better base than Baghdad: one could move in and out freely without visas, residency permits were straightforward, and travel arrangements were infinitely simpler. Simon had been provided with a General Motors four-wheel-drive utility vehicle and elected to drive across the desert from Amman.

The Export Adventurer

We stayed at the Palestine Meridian. To celebrate, we booked a floor-show dinner at the Ishtar Sheraton and secured a table right next to the stage. The entertainment included an excellent dancing troupe from Cairo.

There was a dozen or so girls in the troupe, and during the middle of a particularly energetic can-can routine, the dancer nearest to us was still spinning and kicking in time with the music when, instead of shrieking, she turned toward our table and shouted,

"Simon! What are you doing here?"

Another evening, we were invited to dinner at Tariq's house, and Simon insisted on taking his new brute of a vehicle. Many of Baghdad's streets were hard-packed earth, some of which had recently been excavated and backfilled as part of the city-wide sewer installation. One of the streets near Tariq's house was such a case, and following persistent rain, it had become little more than mud.

Simon was supremely confident that his four-wheel-drive monster would cope. He drove onto the roughly backfilled road and immediately began to sink. There we were, in the middle of an expensive Iraqi suburb, slowly disappearing into the mire, while Simon leafed calmly through the car manual trying to work out how to engage four-wheel drive.

The Export Adventurer

It was a close-run thing. He managed to engage it just before the axles settled into the mud, and after a few forward and backward manoeuvres, the vehicle clawed its way free.

We parked outside Tariq's house and enjoyed a very pleasant evening. When we returned to the vehicle to drive back to the Palestine Meridian, Simon switched on the radio — no reception. There was also a strange whistling noise. It then began to rain, and Simon turned on the windscreen wipers. Nothing happened.

While we were inside Tariq's house, someone had stolen the aerial and the windscreen wiper arms and blades.

Stopped in Kebala for refreshments on the way to Babylon

Over the four years I looked after Iraq, many colleagues joined me on different trips. Because entry visas took three weeks to obtain and an exit visa was required to leave the country, we generally stayed at least a week each time to make the effort worthwhile. That had its compensations, as Fridays were free for touring. We visited Tagit Island, Kerbala, and Babylon, and — rather bizarrely — took photographs of the infamous Abu Ghraib prison.

The Export Adventurer

On three occasions, flights out to Amman were unavailable, and I had to leave Iraq overland by taxi — twice to Amman and once to Kuwait. These journeys were made in elderly American Dodge cars with smooth plastic seats and no air conditioning. The drive from Baghdad to Amman is about 800 kilometres across a rock-strewn, reddish, scorpion-infested desert.

The road is dead straight, disappearing into the shimmering horizon, yet every hour or so you encountered the wreckage of a horrific head-on collision. The crushed hulks were simply pushed to the side of the road. With visibility stretching for miles, the only plausible explanation was driver fatigue.

With Basra closed because of the war with Iran, all supplies had to be brought overland from Amman or via Aleppo in Syria. The route through Rutba and Ramadi was so barren that both Iraq and Jordan had withdrawn their border posts back to the last towns in their territory, leaving nearly 100 kilometres where you were technically in neither country.

Unbelievably, we once encountered a man selling ice cream at the roadside long after passing through Rutba. How he kept it frozen without electricity remains a mystery. The road itself had been so heavily used those overloaded lorries had sunk into the softened tarmac, forming something like railway tracks.

On another journey, George and I headed south toward Kuwait. The Dodge's smooth plastic seat meant we slid sideways every time the driver changed direction. With no air conditioning, closing the windows turned the car into a greenhouse; opening them dehydrated us until our lips cracked.

The Export Adventurer

We stopped at Samawah for lunch. Everything — tables, food, cutlery — was coated in a thick layer of dust. I was resolved not to eat until I saw the cook taking freshly killed small chickens and deep-frying them. I reasoned that a chicken alive moments earlier and then submerged in boiling oil was a reasonably safe bet. It was delicious.

At around five in the afternoon, we reached the junction where the left fork led to Basra and the right to Kuwait. Basra was visible on the horizon, barrage balloons still flying. At the Kuwaiti border, the guards took particular pleasure in confiscating our two-litre bottle of Johnnie Walker Black Label.

Once inside Kuwait, the contrast was startling. Expensive abandoned cars littered the roadsides. In a duty-free oil-rich state, an empty fuel tank or puncture seemed reason enough to abandon a vehicle and buy another. I saw the Kuwait Towers for the first time — water tanks — ironically linked to my very first export project years earlier.

On another occasion, I was due to fly to Kuala Lumpur to meet our CEO for the signing of the Malaysian licence agreement to manufacture our products locally. While still in Iraq, I received an urgent message asking me to phone the office. Expecting the worst, I delayed the call until the next day.

When I finally connected, I learned that my CEO had been made redundant — and I was authorised to sign the licence agreement myself.

Thai Airways had resumed flights from Bangkok to Baghdad, departing from the newly opened Saddam Hussein International Airport. After pushing through the chaotic check-in and security halls, I crossed an air bridge and stepped into the calm, cool serenity of Thai Airways Business Class. The contrast was astonishing.

The Export Adventurer

By early 1982, my 30-page passport was full. The Egyptian Embassy refused me a visa due to lack of space. The British Embassy in Baghdad solved the problem by wiring a new 90-page passport to the old one, resulting in a 120-page travel document that did not expire until 1992.

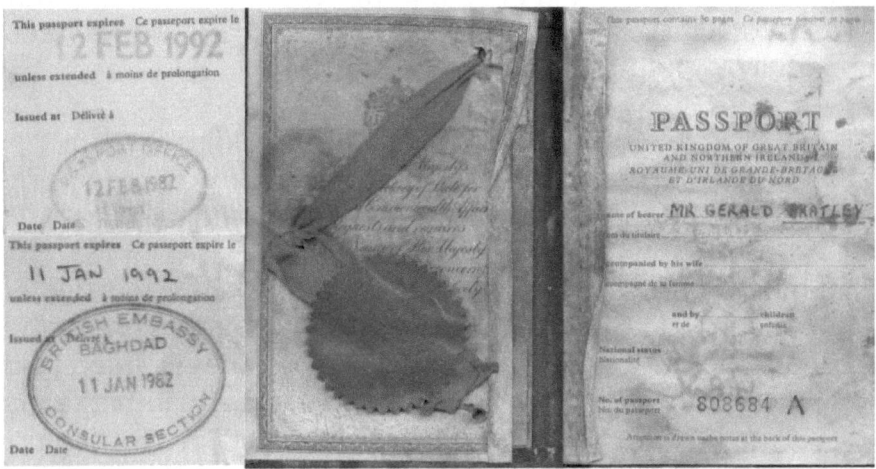

It felt like the perfect end to a remarkable chapter.

Chapter 12 — India

The main reason for visiting India was to follow up with the more than fifty Indian construction contractors working in Iraq. Around twenty were based in Delhi, three or four were dotted around the country, and the other twenty-five were in Bombay — now officially Mumbai, though in those days it answered cheerfully to both.

All the top firms on our target list were in Delhi or Bombay, and the Huddersfield Chamber of Commerce was organising a BOTB-supported trade mission to both cities.

The mission secretary was Keith Welton, Chief Executive of the Huddersfield Chamber. The mission leader was one of the partners from Abbey Anson and Rowe, the Huddersfield architects. However, just before the mission, Keith broke his leg skiing, and the Chamber's export manager, Roger Nunns, had to step in. That unexpected piece of bad luck was the start of an enduring friendship between Roger and me.

As usual, the mission began with the mandatory briefing at the British High Commission in Delhi. It was guarded by Gurkha troops, resplendent in their distinctive uniforms, each with a large sheathed kukri knife hanging from his belt. The High Commissioner talked us through the positives and negatives of India, along with the realities of how business was done.

The next morning, I began my quest: to visit twenty contractors in a single week.

I decided cold-calling was the only way to do it. Appointments sounded civilised, but they would have eaten my whole schedule. I bought a street map of Delhi, plotted every contractor's address, and grouped them so I wasn't zig-zagging pointlessly across the city.

The tactic worked brilliantly — until I hit the suburbs, where finding a taxi between appointments became the real challenge. So, I asked one driver what he would charge to turn his meter off and stay with me all day. He wanted Rs.150 (about £15). It was a no-brainer. From then on, whenever I disappeared into a contractor's office, I knew I had transport waiting when I came out.

New Delhi

Once the driver understood what I was doing, he became part of the operation. While I was inside a meeting, he would work out where the next location was and how to get there. The Indian contractors themselves were delighted to have a visitor from overseas. I was escorted to the right people with impressive efficiency.

Some were called in. Others were woken from naps. Most were somewhere in the building already. And almost without exception they insisted on refreshments — sometimes lovely milky tea, sometimes a bottle of chilled water. Either way, dehydration was not on the agenda.

One firm on my list — Jayprakash Associates — made my life particularly easy. They owned the five-star Delhi hotel we were staying in and had their commercial offices on the second floor. That was one contractor visited without even leaving the building.

I loved travelling from office to office along the teeming streets of old and New Delhi. In old Delhi, around the Red Fort, I witnessed a people-jam for the only time in my life. The market area was so packed that no one could move in any direction. You weren't walking; you were being slowly negotiated forward by the collective body of humanity.

The roads were noisy and crowded. Streets designed and marked out for two lanes of traffic routinely carried four. Holy cows wandered about as if they owned the place — which, in fairness, they more or less did — often followed by goats. Pedestrians crossed the road casually as Leyland buses and Mack trucks weaved around them. Motorbikes, bicycles and pedestrians shared the pavements, which were so uneven that everyone had to watch their footing while still avoiding each other. The three-wheeler "phut phut" taxis performed U-turns and drove against traffic as though it were a minor suggestion rather than a rule.

The air was a constant cacophony: horns, bicycle bells, and the occasional cow bellowing for emphasis.

Amazingly, there were very few accidents. After a time, it became obvious there was a system — an unspoken cooperation. The horns were not blown in anger. They were signals: *beep beep* (watch out, I'm here) and a long continuous blast (I'm in a hurry — please let me through). And people did. If everyone obeyed the written rules strictly, the whole city would have ground to a halt.

The Export Adventurer

The driving would have been seen in the UK as suicidal, yet in India it was tolerated because everyone was watching out for everyone else. It wasn't law that held it together. It was awareness.

At the weekend, Roger organised a bus trip to the Taj Mahal in Agra, about seventy miles from New Delhi. It was magnificent. Anyone who visits India should try to include it.

The following week we travelled to Bombay — Mumbai — where we stayed at the Taj Mahal Hotel, a fabulous super-deluxe place right by the Gateway of India. Once again, I repeated my Delhi tactics and managed to see all but one of the twenty-five contractors in and around Mumbai during the week we were there.

Mumbai again in 2017 & 2018

Mumbai, for me, was a far more vibrant city than Delhi, with more to see and a different energy altogether. The Taj Mahal Hotel and Gateway of India area is the launching point for pleasure cruisers out to Elephanta Island, or across the bay to Navi (New) Mumbai. The Victoria rail terminal, railway station and law court buildings are all in the adjacent Fort area.

It's also a must to visit the shopping streets off Grant Road — with its Thieves Market.

Roger and I hired a horse and carriage and took a tour through the downtown area as far as the red-light district and the market streets. We were horrified to see young women held behind bars. And prostitution was not confined to that district. In the bars of the top hotels, well-dressed middle-aged men with very young women on their arms would openly offer the women for a fee. Once you became aware of the trade, it was easy to spot — and I never saw one of these "arrangements" challenged by hotel staff.

Within a couple of hours of Mumbai there are safari parks, islands and mountainous areas as beautiful as the Lake District.

Chapter 13 — Sri Lanka

Not all the markets I visited yielded very much, and Sri Lanka was one of them. I decided to tag it on to a trade mission to New Delhi and Mumbai. From a purely commercial point of view, the results were modest. I attended several meetings with the Fordham Bathrooms agent, drank a great deal of tea, exchanged much polite optimism — and achieved very little of substance.

Kandy, Sri Lanka

That said, the timing worked in my favour. I was there over a weekend, and the agent, keen to make amends for the lack of business success, insisted on taking me inland to Kandy, up into the mountains. We stayed at the splendid Victoria Hotel, which more than compensated for the thin order book.

The Sri Lankan countryside, especially in the hill country, is extraordinarily beautiful. Lush green valley's fold into one another, terraced paddy fields cling to the slopes, and tiny villages appear everywhere, as if sprinkled deliberately to improve the view. Along the roadsides, locals laid coconut husks directly onto the tarmac, allowing passing traffic to crush and separate the fibres. These were then gathered up and woven into distinctive accessories and garments —

recycling with style and purpose long before it became fashionable.

Working elephants in a Sri Lankan tea plantation

Thanks to my host's local knowledge, I was also taken to visit a tea plantation that still employed a herd of working elephants. Watching these enormous yet gentle creatures pull down small trees and carry massive logs was a privilege. Their calm strength and obvious intelligence made it impossible not to stop and stare.

The plantation itself offered guided tours, and I booked one. The entire party consisted of myself and two young Australian women. We watched workers picking the tea leaves and tipping them into carts, which were then unloaded into a rolling mill that partially crushed the leaves. From there, the leaves were spread about six inches deep on long shelves beneath a curtain of chilled water.

The Export Adventurer

At this stage, the foreman repeatedly scooped up large handfuls of the still-green leaves and sniffed them intently, over and over again, until he was satisfied that enough natural tannic acid had evaporated. Only then were the leaves moved into a machine resembling an industrial tumble dryer, where they were dried.

Next came centrifuges, which separated stalks from leaves and graded the tea into large leaves, small leaves, coarse material and fine dust. We were told the coarse material went into teabags, while most of the fine dust was used to colour cola-type drinks — an unexpected revelation.

At each stage of the process, the tea was emptied directly onto the concrete floor. Bare-chested workers, dressed only in loincloths and glistening with sweat, scooped the leaves from one machine to the next using large aluminium shovels.

The two Australian women grew increasingly uneasy about hygiene. Sensing the tension, I tried to lighten the mood by observing that the saving grace was that you had to pour boiling water over it before you drank it. This did not reassure them. Neither was persuaded to sample the complimentary refreshments offered at the end of the tour.

Back in Colombo, I stayed at a beachside holiday hotel and generally enjoyed the evening entertainment — except for one memorable night. Dining alone at my table, I was suddenly surrounded by a group of six guitar-playing singers who launched enthusiastically into *Island in the Sun*. Being serenaded at close quarters as "Billy No Mates" was not something I found entirely comfortable, and I was relieved when they eventually moved on.

I never minded travelling alone, and for the most part I enjoyed the freedom it brought. But moments like that — standing in a tea plantation, watching elephants at work, or driving through those green mountain valleys — often made me wish that family or friends could have been there to share it.

From Sri Lanka's calm hill country, I moved on to markets that were less picturesque — and far more commercially demanding.

Chapter 14 — The Caribbean

We were approached in London by the Hammerson family, who ran several furniture shops across the capital and the home counties. Alongside this, they had built up a thriving business supplying hotels in the Caribbean with furniture and hotel equipment — a trade that had begun, improbably, as an offshoot of their own holidays. What started as convenience had quietly become commerce. The idea immediately caught my attention, both for the commercial opportunity and for the obvious attraction of the location. When the DTI announced a forthcoming trade mission to Trinidad, I booked a place without hesitation. Charles Hammerson also joined the mission, and with his established local contacts, doors opened almost at once. Once the official programme ended, we continued independently — Barbados, St Lucia, St Vincent, Montserrat, St Kitts and Nevis, and finally Antigua.

It was apparent that the Hammersons were exceptionally well connected throughout the islands. Several builders' merchants agreed to place small stock orders, largely as a trial, to see how the push-fit plumbing system would perform in their local markets.

Over the next two to three years, I managed to justify four separate trips to the Caribbean. Sales grew steadily — never spectacular, but always moving in the right direction. On one occasion, I took my wife with me to Antigua, St Kitts and Nevis. Two economy-class tickets cost no more than a single business-class fare, so as far as the company was concerned, it cost them nothing. Given how often I was away, George approved it without hesitation.

The Export Adventurer

One of the great advantages of travelling with Charles was that he had been to the Caribbean countless times. He knew all the good restaurants, the decent hotels, and the places best avoided. In Trinidad, when we checked into the mission hotel — the Hilton — we were warned very firmly never to attempt walking back from town in the evening. When we asked why, we were told, quite matter-of-factly, that three guests had been murdered doing exactly that within the previous two years. I decided that discretion was the better part of valour and limited my excursions.

Boarding a de-Havilland Otter

We did, however, take a brief diversion to Tobago and spent a Sunday snorkelling over the Bucco Reef — warm water, bright fish and effortless relaxation. In Kingstown, St Vincent, we visited a restaurant run by the legendary Chef Harry, famous not just for his food but for his entertainment. Chef Harry was a portly man, but astonishingly agile, and he demonstrated limbo dancing beneath a bamboo pole set barely a foot off the ground — an improbable but impressive sight.

Arriving in Nevis off the St Kitts Ferry

On another island, we visited beaches with jet-black volcanic sand and took boat trips to hidden caves and luminous blue lagoons. In Barbados, we toured sugar plantations, beaches and Bridgetown. In Nevis, we stayed on the Nisbet Plantation, which was one of the most memorable places of the entire trip.

The plantation consisted of a large house set about a hundred metres back from the ocean, connected to the beach by an avenue of towering coconut palms. The main house held the reception, dining room and bar, while the accommodation was spread across individual bungalows around the estate. In the reception area, there was a large photograph of Prince Charles in swimming attire, walking down the palm-lined avenue towards the sea.

I wandered all over the island with my Olympus OM-10 camera fitted with a large telephoto lens, photographing anything that caught my eye. One day I came across a small house marked with a plaque: it was where Lord Nelson had married Fanny Nisbet. Charles, a committed fitness enthusiast, jogged everywhere and on one occasion took a

The Export Adventurer

Nesbit Plantation house in background

shortcut back to the plantation — only to be chased off neighbouring land by a pack of guard dogs.

On the evening before we were due to leave, I asked the owner of the plantation, Mike Brewer — an Englishman — how he would like to be paid. If he needed Eastern Caribbean dollars, I would need to visit a bank; if he preferred US dollars or sterling, I probably already had enough on me. Mike surprised me by saying, "You don't have to pay. We're all on the same side."

I was completely baffled. After some discussion, it emerged that he preferred English cheques drawn on an English bank. Charles and I both had chequebooks, so that was easily resolved.

Only later did we discover the reason for Mike's generosity. Princess Margaret was due to visit St Kitts and Nevis three weeks later to grant the islands full independence. Mike had assumed — particularly after Prince Charles's visit, combined with my photography and Charles's constant jogging — that we were Special Branch, quietly assessing security arrangements.

The Export Adventurer

Barbados

When I later returned to the Caribbean with my wife, we experienced island travel at its most charmingly chaotic. At the LIAT (Leeward Islands Air Transport) desk, a very large Caribbean lady weighed our luggage, issued our boarding passes and told us to proceed to immigration. We strolled over, where the same lady, now wearing a different hat, checked our passports and waved us on to security. At security, the same woman — hatless this time — picked up yet another hat and scanned our bags.

By the time we reached the departure lounge, we were both highly amused. The lounge itself had no air conditioning and was stiflingly hot, but the large windows were wide open down to about eighteen inches from the floor. Several passengers had stepped outside onto a grassy strip between the lounge and the aircraft apron, so we joined them.

We were waiting for a small Britten-Norman Islander — red and white, with seven seats directly behind the pilot and co-pilot. The lady with the hats reappeared, pointed at a tiny black speck in the sky and announced, "That is your flight now."

On another occasion at the same tiny Nevis airport, a slightly larger de Havilland Otter landed and taxied in. About thirty passengers disembarked in a state of visible distress — some crying, others praying aloud. We wondered what disaster had occurred until a coffin emerged from the tail of the aircraft.

The Export Adventurer

Another memorable flight occurred with Charles in St Lucia. We were at Castries Airport early one morning to catch the first flight of a new airline, Winair, bound for St Vincent. Charles and I were the only two passengers and sat directly behind the pilots. Shortly after take-off, while still climbing, the pilot turned around and asked if we were in a hurry. When we said we were not — our appointments wouldn't start before ten — he replied that he was pleased, as he needed a coffee.

He altered course, radioed the tower at Hewanorra Airport on the other side of the island, landed, taxied to a hardstanding some two hundred metres from the terminal and told us to return in thirty minutes. He and the co-pilot disappeared in the opposite direction. Charles and I climbed over barriers to get into the terminal, unchallenged, bought coffee, then climbed back out again — still unchallenged. We arrived in St Vincent an hour late, none the worse for it.

In St Kitts, we stayed at Watling's Plantation. In Antigua, we spent many pleasant days around Nelson's Dockyard and English Harbour. With the Caribbean's laid-back work ethic, weekends were sacrosanct: five days of business followed by two days on the beach, drinking white rum and coke or heading out on a small pleasure craft, cooling off in the spray.

Business may have been modest, but the experiences were anything but.

From the relaxed informality of the Caribbean, I moved on to markets where nothing — from time to trust — came quite so easily.

Chapter 15 — Jordan

Jordan was a market I already knew well from my Bratley Newton Associates days and from my first visit after joining Bartol–Hepworth. On returning, I looked up my old agent, George Baddour. George was of Palestinian origin but a practising Christian, and although the Palestinian refugee camps still existed in the Jordan Valley, he steered well clear of politics. It was wise. Jordan survived as a calm oasis in a turbulent region largely because people knew when not to talk.

One of the very first projects I had worked on at BNA was the Aqaba Holiday Inn with Emile Jouzy. Over the years, I ploughed a great deal of effort into Jordan, but the rewards were always modest. Still, it remained an important base — and a place of respite.

When I was paying the bills myself at Bratley Newton Associates, I stayed in a small family-run hotel just down the hill from the luxurious Amman Intercontinental, on the parallel road near the Third Circle. The numbered "circles" marked the main roundabouts radiating out from the city centre — by my last visit they were up to six. I stayed often at the City Hotel and became friendly with the owner and his adult sons.

The Export Adventurer

At the City Hotel you had a simple choice. If your room faced the main road, you would be woken at 6 a.m. by traffic. If it faced the rear, you would be awake at 5 a.m. by the call to prayer from a nearby mosque. Either way, sleep was optional.

One Friday they invited me to go hunting with them. I readily agreed — it beat sitting around the hotel all day. We drove out into semi-desert scrubland to hunt pigeons. I was astonished when rifles were handed out: everyone received a .22 except the hotel owner, who carried a small sub-machine gun. To this day, I am not entirely sure whether that was meant as a joke for my benefit or whether he was quite serious.

One of Jordan's great virtues — surrounded as it was by conflict in Israel, Lebanon and Syria — was its stability under King Hussein. After Iraq, it became a place of recovery. Whether you had fought your way onto an aircraft or endured a fourteen-hour overland desert journey, you needed a day or two in Amman to decompress.

In the city centre, near the Philadelphia Hotel, sat the Roman amphitheatre, surrounded by markets and second-hand shops. But Jordan's real attractions lay beyond the city. The Dead Sea was less than an hour away. Petra — carved entirely from red sandstone — was unforgettable. Jerash offered a complete Roman city: streets, forum, temples and two amphitheatres. Madaba held its ancient mosaic map of the Middle East, and Mount Nebo offered the view from which Moses is said to have seen the Promised Land.

Over the years, I visited Petra and Jerash several times, floated in the Dead Sea on many occasions, and saw the rest at least once. It was also in Amman that I discovered Middle Eastern honey-and-pistachio baklava. Jabri's cake and coffee shop sticks vividly in my memory, and I often wonder whether it still exists.

One of my strangest flight experiences also occurred in Jordan. It was early May, and I had a confirmed booking on the 2 p.m. Royal Jordanian (Alia) flight from Amman to London. At around 8 a.m., I walked out of the Amman Intercontinental to buy a copy of the *Jordan Herald*. As I stepped onto the forecourt, a Royal Jordanian Boeing 747 flew low overhead.

At the time, Royal Jordanian was transitioning from Boeing 707s to 747s and had only two of them — one on the Bangkok route and one on the London route. I was booked on the London aircraft. I felt instantly uneasy. There was a fifty-percent chance my flight had already departed.

I went straight back to my room, collected my ticket and  headed for the Royal Jordanian sales office in the hotel. They explained that my travel agent had used the old schedule; all flight times had changed on May 1st. Because Royal Jordanian and British Airways pooled the route, only one airline flew the Amman–London sector each day. Ordinarily, that would have meant waiting until the following day.

However, the staff told me British Airways was operating an additional flight that evening and might accept my ticket. They endorsed it, and I went directly to the BA office — conveniently located in the same hotel.

The BA staff laughed when I asked if there was space and then asked where I would like to sit. I thought nothing of it at the time; I was simply relieved to be getting home on schedule.

At Queen Alia Airport — named after King Hussein's English-born wife — the BA flight arrived from Doha. The Lockheed TriStar departed on time. Shortly after take-off, I realised the significance of that earlier question. There were only six passengers on an aircraft built for over three hundred.

The Export Adventurer

The captain announced that, because this was a special flight with so few passengers, meals and drinks would be served on request rather than to a schedule. There were more crew than passengers. We could have whatever we wanted, whenever we wanted it.

By the time I was on my second gin and tonic, a stewardess appeared offering champagne. When I queried this, she explained that the BA station manager in Doha was retiring and this was his final flight to London — a celebration of his twenty-five years with the airline.

It seemed a fitting gesture, but the real surprise came on arrival at Heathrow. After an exceptionally smooth landing, while taxiing to the terminal, the captain announced that we had just experienced the first fully automated, computer-controlled landing ever performed by a British commercial aircraft.

And I had been there to witness it — one of six passengers, blissfully unaware until the very end.

From Jordan's calm pragmatism, my travels soon carried me onward again — into markets where certainty was rarer and improvisation once more became essential.

Chapter 16 — Egypt

I only visited Cairo a couple of times, largely because we already had an office and resident representatives in the market. On my first visit, I arrived on Kuwait Airways. As we departed Kuwait, I found myself quietly amused while the stewardess went through the safety procedures. Once we were airborne and she had served me a drink (a soft drink—Kuwait does not permit alcohol), she asked why I had been smiling.

I explained that it was because she had been demonstrating the lifejacket. She asked why I found that amusing, so I replied by asking how much water we actually flew over between Kuwait and Cairo. She saw the humour immediately and went off to share it with her colleagues.

I checked into the Heliopolis Intercontinental Hotel, contacted Simon and Phil in our Cairo office, and arranged to meet them in the bar of the Nile Hilton at 7 p.m. The bar was full of British expatriates drinking locally brewed Amstel beer, which—mysteriously—seemed to have a much higher alcohol content than the Amstel available in Europe. We had a very pleasant evening, and they persuaded me to move from the Intercontinental to the Hilton, which I did the following day.

Once again, I had timed my visit well. It was Friday, and I went off to have tea and cakes at the Mina House Hotel—the famous old hotel featured in Agatha Christie's books—before heading out to the pyramids and the Sphinx at Giza. From one side, the site opens onto a vast desert vista, but if you walk around to the other, you can photograph the pyramids with the suburbs of Cairo clearly visible in the background.

The Export Adventurer

Seeing the pyramids and the Sphinx was a treat, although I must admit that Petra is far more impressive.

While exploring the city, I was walking down Qasr El Nil Street when I came across a shoe shop advertising made-to-measure footwear. I enquired about the price, which turned out to be less than I had recently paid in Hong Kong for the same service, so I placed an order. The shoes were ready the following day. Sensibly, I decided to test them before leaving Cairo and wore them over the next couple of days. They were comfortable and held their shape well.

Unfortunately, back in the UK I was caught in a shower while wearing them, and it soon became clear that the glue used was water-based. As I walked along, the shoes began to fall apart.

Shortly afterwards, I received a message from head office asking when I would be back, as our Scandinavian agent, Stephen Guise in Copenhagen, had a contractor in Helsinki with a technical issue that required urgent attention. The plan was for me to return to the UK, collect a member of our technical staff, and escort him to Helsinki.

I checked the available flights and found a KLM service from Cairo to Amsterdam via Athens, which suited me perfectly. There were far better onward connections from Amsterdam to Leeds/Bradford or Humberside than from Heathrow.

The Export Adventurer

I set off still wearing my new Egyptian made-to-measure shoes.

The aircraft turned out to be surprisingly small—a Fokker F28 Fellowship. On take-off, it did not so much bank to the left as throw itself into a very steep turn, clearly intent on avoiding overflying Cairo. The angle was so acute that I found myself wondering whether the pilot had spent most of his earlier career flying fighter jets and had momentarily forgotten that the rest of us were not strapped into ejection seats.

When we arrived in Athens, passengers were allowed to disembark while the aircraft was refuelled. We were instructed to return to the boarding gate within forty-five minutes. After half an hour, an announcement was made:

"Will all passengers for KLM flight XYZ please proceed to the restaurant."

Restaurant? I thought. If they are feeding you, you are in for a long delay. There was no point worrying, so I relaxed and enjoyed the free meal. After another hour, just as I was finishing dessert, a further announcement followed:

"Will all passengers for KLM flight XYZ please proceed to Gate 23 for immediate boarding."

Joy. Only an hour's delay—and a free meal thrown in.

We boarded again, with new passengers joining us. After take-off, the pilot once more executed an impressively steep bank to avoid overflying Athens. The man sitting next to me remarked, "I bet he flew Spitfires before he joined KLM."

Once we reached cruising altitude, the pilot came on the intercom. He explained that he understood we were all wondering why we had first been fed and then rushed back onto the aircraft. The reason, he said, was that the primary radar had failed on the Cairo–Athens leg, and it had been hoped it could be replaced in Athens.

Unfortunately, the required part was not available. The options were either to wait for a replacement to be flown in from Amsterdam or to obtain permission to fly "blind" and be talked through the route sector by sector by ground control. He had secured the necessary permissions from all controllers along the way and had chosen the latter option.

I did wonder how many of us would have boarded had we known that beforehand.

Arriving back from Cairo's pleasant January temperature of around 20°C, I spent the following day in the office and then flew that evening into a temperature of –30°C in Helsinki.

On my second visit to Cairo, I was accompanied by George Bell. We were walking along one of the streets in the city centre when George spotted a shop selling leather trench coats. His eyes lit up, and he dragged me inside. He asked the price and was impressed by how low it was. They did not have his size in stock but assured him they could make one to measure within a day.

As we still had a day and a half left in Cairo, George decided to go ahead. He then turned to me and said, "You're getting one too, Gerry."

I protested that I didn't want one, but George insisted. I went along with it, wondering why he wanted us both to look like Gestapo officers. When we left the shop, I asked him why he wanted matching coats. He explained that he had always

The Export Adventurer

wanted a leather coat like the ones worn by Swiss border guards.

I asked why I needed one.

His reply was simple:

"Both coats are going on your expenses."

When we left Cairo, I flew back to London, and George went on to Brussels via Frankfurt, wearing his Swiss border-guard coat. I never saw him wear it again.

From Cairo, I moved on to Lebanon, where recent destruction had shifted attention almost entirely toward reconstruction and the rapid replacement of buildings and infrastructure.

Chapter 17 — Lebanon

Soon after Israeli forces launched their invasion of Lebanon on 6 June 1982 and smashed through the longstanding Green Line that had divided East and West Beirut, we began considering how we might take part in what was clearly going to be a massive rebuilding programme. One of the directors at Hepworth Ceramic Holdings (HCH) contacted us to say he was joining a trade mission with the Minister for Trade that was expected to include Beirut. That information sharpened our interest, and we carried out some preliminary work with HCH. When the mission failed to materialise, I decided to add Beirut to my next itinerary and see the situation for myself. In our research, we turned up a construction company interested in becoming our agents in Lebanon. So, I made arrangements to visit Beirut.

I flew into Beirut airport on the Lebanese carrier Middle Eastern Airlines. The first impression was dreadful as we descended from the aircraft and climbed down the steps onto the tarmac where two wide airport shuttle buses were waiting. The buses had bullet holes in some of the panels, and quite a few windows were missing.

When we approached the terminal building, part of it was still covered in smoke stains where it had been on fire, and there were holes and damage everywhere. There were many more signs of war damage inside the terminal building.

Once through the airport, I went to the taxi rank and waited in line, and after a few minutes, I was at the front of the queue. I had been watching the policeman taking down the details from every passenger's passport, the driver's name, and the registration number of the taxi they used. I thought it was a bit officious at the time. However, when Terry Waite, John

McCarthy, Brian Keenan, and over a hundred others started to be kidnapped just a few weeks after I returned from Beirut, I was glad of the extra security.

The whole of the area outside the airport was severely damaged. Most houses had no windows or doors; many were partially destroyed; many were totally destroyed. However, there was lots of evidence of repairs. Some concrete buildings had already been patched up; others had shuttering in position ready for new pours; and many more were half-collapsed—concrete slabs sitting at forty-five degrees to the earth—yet still occupied, with electric lighting shining from within the hulks.

Water was bubbling up from the ground everywhere, from ruptured water supply pipes—damage created by the shockwaves of bombs.

Within half a mile of the airport, we came across traffic circling counterclockwise on the red earth. I asked the driver why they were circling in this way, and he told me that until three weeks earlier, there had been a roundabout on that site. There was no sign of tarmac, kerbstones, or anything else that would have hinted that such a large structure had ever existed. It had been totally wiped off the face of the earth.

The Export Adventurer

We drove through the wrecked city centre. All the buildings were utterly blackened, burnt-out gutted shells; most had no roofs, windows, or doors. Those that had retained their roller shutters over doors and windows were so perforated with bullet holes that it was impossible to put your hand on one without covering at least one hole. Side streets were cordoned off with skull-and-crossbones signs warning of mines.

I was heading for an address near the Bain Militare (military baths) near the Ferris wheel on the seafront. When I arrived, I saw that the area was mostly intact.

I was welcomed by Mr Khatib, who took me out for dinner, spending most of the time on the way there and back pointing out the worst damage. We arrived at a restaurant on the promenade just outside the wrecked city centre. Lebanese food—baklava, falafel, taramasalata, hummus, kafta, tabbouleh—and eating it with pita bread, washed down with arak, is one of my favourite ways of eating. We ordered and sat looking out onto the Mediterranean below us. Halfway through the meal, there were the sounds of gunfire nearby, and the staff whisked us away around the back of a bullet-proof wall, where we continued our meal.

I did a lot of walking in the daytime in what I was told were the safe areas and came across a shop on Alhambra Street which had just reopened after four years, selling Pringle sweaters.

The Export Adventurer

The price they wanted made me suspicious of their true origin, so I bought one and had it laundered to see how it performed. That was Friday. On Saturday, I flew to Cyprus, where I had the sweater laundered, and returned to Beirut on Wednesday. I made a beeline for the shop to buy more sweaters at the four-year-old prices. Unfortunately, when I got there, it had disappeared. It had been blown up during the time I was away.

While in Beirut, I bought an Arabic bubble pipe with full-leaf tobacco and special tablets for lighting the tobacco ball. The shop owner asked me several times if I wanted anything else but, preoccupied, I did not think much about his question at the time. However, when I was in the queue for customs inspection at Heathrow, I started to worry whether "anything else" might already be in my parcel—because Beirut was famous for its wacky backy. I need not have worried, but it reinforced the necessity of packing everything yourself.

Mr Khatib spent quite a lot of time with me. He took me to the casino area north of the city, which was totally undamaged and fully operational. I also asked him to take me to the Hilton Hotel, where I had sold firefighting equipment a few years earlier. The Christian Phalangists had used the building to fire at the Druze. The counterattack set the hotel alight, and it burned down with the extinguishers and firefighting equipment still trapped in the docks. It was like all the other city centre buildings: a windowless, perforated black hulk.

I never saw Beirut before the Civil War, when Arab playboys used the city and its casinos for their enjoyment. There are estimates that over three thousand ladies of the night were in residence then.

Alas, we never got a look in. French standards were the dominant specifications for the replacement utilities, so we were effectively precluded from tendering.

Chapter 18 — Malaysia

As the newly appointed Export Development Manager, it was a hectic period. I flew out to Malaysia to assess the opportunity for cooperation, and from the outset it was clear that the prospects were excellent.

The Plastics Centre (SDN) Berhad was the largest manufacturer of plastic products in Malaysia. They supplied bottles to Smith & Nephew, mudguards and plastic components to the Honda motorcycle factory, and television and radio casings for local manufacturers and assemblers. Their facilities included blow moulding, extrusion, injection moulding and vacuum forming, so producing our soil, waste and drainage pipes was well within their technical capabilities.

George and I with the Malaysian team

They brought in one of the local directors of Bayer, along with a specialist who had already been involved with a competitor's plastic pipes and fittings operation. I negotiated a licence with them to manufacture the pipes. They paid a modest US$50,000 down payment to offset the costs we would incur in providing drawings and technical assistance. In addition, they agreed to pay a 5 per cent running royalty on the sales value of all pipes manufactured, and to purchase all fittings from our UK factories. From first discussions to signing the contract took no more than two or three trips.

The Sng family and the launch plan

The Sng family, who owned The Plastics Centre (SDN) Berhad, had recently lost their patriarch. The eldest son, Michael—then in his mid-thirties—took over the business, assisted by his brothers Geoffrey and Raymond. They had been approached by Steve Yeow, who had been involved in launching the Terrain product range in Malaysia, and they also brought in a marketing executive from Bayer Malaysia, Mr Steve Young.

The initial plan was that Steve Yeow would leave the competitor and take over as general manager of the new plastic pipe and fittings company, later named Bina-Bartol. That did not come to pass, and instead Steve Yeow travelled to the UK to meet with us.

During a series of meetings in Doncaster, the Malaysians asked whether I would help them launch the business in Malaysia. The timing was opportune. We were closing our Cairo office. Simon had already moved to Amman to cover Jordan and Iraq, and George was looking for another role for Phil, the remaining Cairo employee.

We discussed the implications at length. If I relocated to Malaysia, I would become Export Manager for the Far East and Australasia, covering the entire region from a Kuala Lumpur base. The Malaysians were prepared to contribute an additional £10,000 per annum toward my salary and to cover all local housing costs. Bartol would continue paying my UK salary on a registered expatriate basis, free of UK tax. Bartol UK would cover my expenses outside Malaysia, while The

Plastics Centre (SDN) Berhad would meet all costs incurred within Malaysia.

I would not accept the post unless my wife and family came with me. That meant return air tickets twice a year for the whole family. My youngest son was still at school, so they also agreed to cover school fees at the British School in Kuala Lumpur.

Family life, and the cost of distance

All this upheaval came at a difficult time for my wife. Her mother, who had been unwell but appeared to be improving, encouraged her to go, talking about the chance to see the world and a once-in-a-lifetime opportunity. In the end, we all flew out to Kuala Lumpur except our eldest daughter, Jayne (18). So off we went: Paul, Jason, my wife and me.

Jason took some time to settle into the British School. His UK education lagged behind their curriculum, and we had to pay for extra tuition to help him catch up—exactly what Jason least wanted at that age.

Over the first few months, Paul—then sixteen—was at a loose end, and I was arranging for him to join us in the Bina-Bartol office when my wife received devastating news from home. Her mother had been diagnosed with terminal cancer, and she returned to the UK immediately.

Paul and Jason stayed with me. My wife came back after a couple of weeks, but under the circumstances she could never truly settle.

My family being entertained by the Palmco staff at the Kasserina Beach in Penang

When she returned, we managed a few weekend trips—down to the beaches in Malacca. Palmco, our local Bina-Bartol agents in Penang, owned the Kassarina Beach Hotel and kindly invited my family for a short break. My wife famously—and bravely—went paragliding. We were exceptionally well looked after, wined and dined by senior hotel staff and Palmco management.

But her mother's condition deteriorated rapidly, and Jeanie was desperate to remain close to her. We therefore decided that she and the boys would return to the UK. We would use the married-status return tickets built into my contract to bring them out twice a year on holiday, and I would get home as often as possible.

Living almost permanently apart, my wife and I—married for nearly twenty years—began to drift. I did bring her and the children out twice: once to Kuala Lumpur and on to my brothers in Sydney, and once to Hong Kong and Seoul. But it was too little, too late, and our marriage eventually foundered.

Settling in: visas, phones, and early "email"

It took time to secure my Malaysian residency visa and work permit, so for the first six months I had to fly to Singapore every month, stay overnight, and return the following day.

The Export Adventurer

Communications were in transition. Telex was giving way to facsimile, and very early email was just beginning to appear. I carried a Psion mini-computer, which I could connect to hotel telephone lines and use to send emails. It was primitive: the connection ran through CompuServe on a 64-bps dial-up modem, and sending even a short message took an age.

International telephone calls—especially from hotels—were prohibitively expensive and avoided whenever possible. Malaysia also suffered from a shortage of telephone lines, and it took nearly a year for a landline to be installed in my apartment.

I initially lived at Fairview Mansions, later moving to the Faber Ria condominium, both on Old Kelang Road (Jalan Kelang Lama) just outside Kuala Lumpur on the Petaling Jaya side—close to The Plastics Centre headquarters.

Faber Ria was an excellent place to live. The apartment had three large bedrooms, a spacious lounge-kitchen and two bathrooms, on the lift-served third floor, with reserved underground parking. The complex included a half-size Olympic swimming pool, laundry, restaurant and bar. There were six other British expatriates living there, and we met most evenings in the bar.

The Falklands War broke out while I was living at Faber Ria. One of the British expatriates was particularly anxious because his son was serving aboard the requisitioned North Sea Ferries *Norland* en route to Port Stanley.

BAS, TEKSI, and "DADA MEANS DEATH"

One of the first things visitors notice in Malaysia is the lingering influence of British colonial administration on the language.

When the Latin alphabet was adopted in 1947, many English words were phonetically respelled. The two most noticeable were BAS for BUS and TEKSI for TAXI—both displayed prominently on vehicles throughout the country. It could be mildly irritating when you were going "haime" for some bread and "batter".

Every landing card—completed by everyone entering or leaving Malaysia—also carried a warning in bold red lettering:

DADA MEANS DEATH
(DADA = drugs)

It was not something you forgot.

George in Malaysia: peanuts, morphine, and a windsurfer

George visited me in Malaysia on several occasions. On one trip we went up to the Genting Highlands and Fraser's Hill. On the way back I bought some locally roasted peanuts and immediately realised—after the first one—that something was very wrong. I spat out what I could.

Too late. I had ingested enough to spend the next seventy-two hours suffering the worst bout of vomiting and diarrhoea I have ever experienced. George went in search of kaolin-and-morphine medicine and later told me he was almost arrested because morphine and other opiates are strictly controlled in Malaysia. And there, in red, on the landing card, was the reminder: *DADA MEANS DEATH.*

On another visit, George and I went down to the beach I had discovered with my family in Malacca. George hired a windsurfer and I hired a sailing dinghy. We spent a wonderful day skimming up and down the coastline, stepping straight into fully rigged craft and sailing off, then returning them to the attendants to de-rig.

Malaysia was sheer paradise.

Building the business: people first, then pipe

Our plastic pipe factory was located on an industrial estate north of Kuala Lumpur, just off the Ipoh Road. Each day I passed the Moorish architecture of Kuala Lumpur railway station and the famous Batu Caves.

Malaysia comprises three distinct cultures: the Bumiputera (the original Indo-Malay population), who are constitutionally guaranteed control of government; the Chinese, who own most of the businesses; and the Tamil Indians, who operate many of the shops. Fortunately for me, English was both the official language and the language of business.

While the factory was under construction and the extrusion machines were on order, I advertised for, interviewed, appointed and trained the sales force. We entered the market before production began, calling on architects, consulting engineers and major contractors throughout the region. Sub-agents were appointed in Penang and in East Malaysia—Sabah and Sarawak in Borneo. We were fully operational by the time the first pipe was produced.

Technical staff from HQ supported us, though they initially struggled to achieve the required standards because the adjustments necessary for production in a tropical environment were far from trivial.

This led to one memorable episode. We were instructed to send one kilogram of local white PVC resin powder to the UK for analysis. DHL and TNT initially refused to transport a kilo of white powder—quite reasonably interpreting "white powder" as *DADA*. After verification and explanation, DHL eventually agreed to ship it.

Life in KL: fast, easy, cheap… and lost spectacles

Shopping in Kuala Lumpur was effortless. You could fill a supermarket trolley, give the cashier your address and the time you would be home, and the groceries would be delivered to your door—payment on delivery.

Downtown, Sungai Wang Plaza was a vast shopping mall. My sons loved browsing the watches, jewellery and electronics. Paul needed new spectacles, chose frames, and had them ready within hours.

The following day we went to Malacca, and Paul forgot he was wearing them when he dived off a boat into the sea. We were back at the opticians the next day.

Everything was quick, easy and usually inexpensive.

Jason and I once visited the Shah Alam Formula One circuit to watch Australian Superbike racing. As Europeans, we were allowed to wander freely and spent most of the day in and around the pits.

Restaurants, Louis XIII, and tiger prawns

When I was alone in Kuala Lumpur, Michael and Geoffrey Sng often took me out. They were wealthy men with a taste for fine food and brandy.

Each time I travelled out of Malaysia they asked me to buy a bottle of Rémy Martin Louis XIII in the Hong Kong duty-free shop. At the time it cost around US$750 for a 70cl bottle—far cheaper than in Kuala Lumpur. I would bring it back, be reimbursed immediately, and off we would go to a top restaurant to drink it.

One favourite venue was an outdoor garden restaurant behind the KL Hilton, on the land later occupied by the Petronas Towers. My favourite dish there was giant drunken tiger prawns.

The prawns arrived alive in a metal bowl. Alcohol was poured over them, then either added to a charcoal-heated steamboat or ignited directly, cooking the prawns in flames. They changed colour from green-blue to pink almost instantly, the transformation racing down their fifteen-inch antennae like fireworks.

They delighted in testing my culinary limits. Over time I ate vampire bat (rather like hare), flying fox, a bear's arm complete with inch-long claws, sea slug, sea cucumber and century eggs—raw eggs preserved until the white becomes smoky jelly and the yolk turns black.

I became particularly fond of *Bak Kut Teh*—pork bone tea—a Hokkien soup infused with herbs, loaded with pork ribs, garlic, mushrooms and tofu puffs, served with rice and oolong tea.

Michael and Geoffrey also introduced me to a Japanese lounge bar with large low tables surrounded by couchettes. A young woman would join each customer, pour drinks, peel fruit, converse and dance if required.

They also took me to health clubs where young masseuses worked in open rooms with multiple tables. On one occasion, after half an hour of massage, my masseuse climbed onto my back and began walking across it with bare feet.

"This has been a problem all my life," I joked.

Michael looked concerned. "Why, Gerry—what is the problem?"

"Women have always walked all over me," I replied.

Heat, rain, durian, and expat life

Kuala Lumpur lies three degrees north of the equator. There are no seasons, only the monsoon in July and August, when rain can fall all day. The rest of the year it rains almost every evening at dusk as warm air cools and moisture condenses.

The temperature hovered around 82°F, plus or minus two degrees. Air conditioning was essential. Fresh tropical fruit was always available, including durian—delicious custard-like flesh with a smell so offensive that most Asian airlines banned it from their aircraft.

My marriage was by then in serious trouble, and like several other expatriates at Faber Ria, I began spending more time in bars and at apartment parties. Alcohol and excess became normalised.

Doncaster problems, "Ken", and losing face

While I was in Malaysia, Bartol in Doncaster descended into chaos. Managing director Brian Davies, who had replaced Mike Marsden, was moved on. Bob Anderson was imposed by Hepworth Ceramic Holdings as the third CEO in as many years. He arrived with his sales and marketing lieutenant—whom I shall call Ken.

Peter Marshall retired, and Ken replaced both Peter in home sales and George Bell in export. George was sidelined and returned to head the technical department.

I spent far too much time briefing successive executives. After six to nine months, Bob Anderson collapsed on a train en route to an HCH board meeting and was hospitalised with a suspected heart attack.

Ken somehow survived into the next regime and retained control of export. He understood nothing about exporting and could not make decisions. His favourite phrase was:

"I've got lots of balls in the air, and I don't know how they'll come down."

He visited Malaysia and immediately conceded a further five per cent discount on fittings after two years of careful negotiation. That destroyed Bartol-Hepworth's margin—and made me lose face. In Asian culture, that damage is permanent.

"DADA MEANS DEATH" strikes again: customs and a container

A forty-foot container arrived with pricing errors that caused import duties to be overpaid. An attempt to correct the imbalance on the next shipment resulted in items being omitted from the invoice altogether.

Customs accused us of smuggling and threatened confiscation and penalties ten times the invoice value. After days of negotiation, a senior official agreed to release the goods in exchange for £1,000 in cash as "compensation".

Ken later congratulated me—and asked whether I could get a receipt.

We laughed helplessly.

The move to Seoul

I remained in Malaysia for two years, until South Korea required more attention and I was spending more time in Seoul than Kuala Lumpur. I was also negotiating a licensing agreement in New Zealand.

Both licences involved the Bartol polybutylene Acorn push-fit hot and cold water system—a far more complex product requiring extrusion, injection moulding and precision components.

New Zealand could be managed through visits and telecommunications. South Korea could not.

The Export Adventurer

So, I moved my residence to Seoul, continuing to visit Kuala Lumpur each month.

Chapter 19 — West Africa

Nigeria

Wolverhampton Chamber of Commerce announced that they were organising a trade mission to Nigeria. The country had slowly recovered from the Biafran War, and we had a live reason to go: Tarmac West Africa had contacted us for a consignment of 4-inch drainage fittings which—according to our records—should already have been in stock in Lagos at our stockist, Tate & Lyle. We shipped the fittings required, but as no one had visited Tate & Lyle for some considerable time, I decided to join the mission to Nigeria and use the opportunity to assess other nearby markets as well.

After some research, we identified The Gambia, Ghana and Sierra Leone as the three most likely markets, largely because they still specified British Standard products. However, we had recently enjoyed some success with our push-fit 15 mm and 22 mm water supply system in France, and we wondered whether that could be replicated across parts of the surrounding Francophone nations—Côte d'Ivoire, Togo, Senegal and Liberia.

Most of the participants flew from Birmingham, connecting with KLM via Amsterdam to Lagos. I was the odd one out, choosing Leeds to Amsterdam and then joining the group at Schiphol arrivals. In Amsterdam, however, the Wolverhampton Chamber's lady travel agent—who had travelled with the main group—arranged for KLM to meet me at the gate as I stepped off the Air UK flight. I was whisked through baggage and hustled onto the coach, catching up with my fellow mission members as though I'd been part of the convoy all along.

The Export Adventurer

We stayed overnight at an airport hotel. After freshening up, some of the group elected to take the tram into central Amsterdam to see the sights. About ten of us went. We got off at Dam Square, only a few hundred yards from the infamous canal-side red-light district. One or two in the party clearly knew their way around, and before long we were in a theatre watching a live sex show.

It was an unusual way to meet new people, but it certainly broke the ice. Export salespeople tend to be extroverts—otherwise they wouldn't survive either the competitive cut and thrust of the work, or the rigours of travel and living out of a suitcase for weeks at a time.

It also became clear why the travel agent had travelled with us as far as Amsterdam. She cosied up to one mission member and I definitely heard the question—"my room or yours?"—on the tram ride back to the hotel.

Our flight was at 11 a.m., so there was no early-morning scramble: a leisurely breakfast, repack the case, and back onto the coach.

When we arrived in Lagos, a member of the British High Commission commercial team met us at the airport, collected all our passports and luggage tags, and ushered us straight onto the coach. Immigration, baggage collection and customs clearance were effectively handled for us. We reached the Echo Holiday Inn on Bar Beach in time for dinner and a few drinks.

We had all been allocated twin rooms—shared with fellow mission members.

The first morning we were taken to the British High Commission for a briefing by the High Commissioner.

The Export Adventurer

Attendance was mandatory: both the opening briefing and the final debrief were part of the subvention conditions.

One point the High Commissioner emphasised was the risk of theft and mugging.

A car sent from Tate & Lyle collected me from the High Commission and took me across town to their offices. The general manager, Mr Gordon Mango, and the two managers responsible for the plastic pipe and fittings business were waiting. We had a good discussion, and it was clear they already knew there were problems.

We worked through the specific issue Tarmac had experienced obtaining fittings from the stock point. I was assured that measures had been put in place to ensure it did not happen again.

I asked Gordon how serious the crime risk really was. He confirmed it was high and recommended that I never leave the hotel unless I was in a group or in a car. He also advised me not to leave valuables in the room, as daytime break-ins were common.

Back at the hotel, I locked most of my money and travel documents in the safe. Whenever I left my room, I locked anything else of value inside my briefcase, then locked the briefcase inside my Samsonite suitcase—and hid the suitcase under the bed.

Outside the guarded hotel gates there was always a crowd of girls of ill repute. Their standard method of attracting attention—especially when you were in a car—was to hiss loudly. One mission member remarked after dinner one night that it was the only place in the world he'd been where the STDs announced their presence.

The Export Adventurer

Later in the week I returned to the hotel to collect something from my room. While I was there, I heard a key in the lock and assumed it was the maid. Instead, a smartly dressed, middle-aged West African man appeared, key in hand, standing in the doorway. His surprise mirrored my own. He apologised quickly, said he must be on the wrong floor, and beat a hasty retreat before I could collect my thoughts.

It could have been a genuine mistake—but it was far more likely an attempted burglary.

Tate & Lyle arranged for me to visit almost every major user of plastic pipes and fittings in Lagos. The lack of stock kept coming up, so I asked if I could visit the stock point.

When I saw the warehouse, I examined the fittings carefully. They had every combination: straight couplings, bends, reducers, tees, connectors to salt-glaze pipes, access bends (bends with a rodding point)—every size from 1¼ inch through to six inches.

Tarmac's specific problem was a fitting they couldn't obtain locally: a six-inch tee with a four-inch branch.

Tate & Lyle had no 6 × 6 × 4 tees in stock.

But they did have several hundred six-inch equal tees—and nearly a thousand 6 × 4 reducers.

It had never occurred to them that combining the two fittings would produce exactly the required result.

It was, quite simply, a training issue. When I left, Gordon Mango was already organising a programme.

The Export Adventurer

Lagos itself was dusty and built-up: elevated roads and modern buildings mixed with lean-to shanties. Pedestrian crossings were painted, but few people used them, and motorists certainly paid them no attention.

Every now and then you would see a dead body lying by the roadside.

One morning I felt genuinely sick when I saw what looked like a teenage boy in a pristine school uniform lying dead in the gutter. The traffic carried on as usual.

Public executions by firing squad were still carried out on Bar Beach on most Sundays. So Fred—the export manager of the Wolverhampton Chamber—arranged for those who wanted a "better" beach to hire a boat and go to a nearby one. I went.

Although it was a small island, it had deckchairs and windbreaks for hire, a constant supply of drinks (alcoholic and non-alcoholic), ice cream—and, crucially, ice.

When we got back to the hotel, my roommate went to his briefcase and found both hasps broken off. All his money and valuables were gone. He was devastated—but despite the High Commission briefing, and despite my story about the man unlocking my door, he had taken no precautions.

One mission member carried two newspaper cuttings in his market notes. The first, from *The Times*, reported that the second-largest vessel in the Nigerian Navy had sailed from Lagos and run into difficulties somewhere off the Isles of Scilly. The Navy had asked the Royal Navy for assistance and were meanwhile investigating who was responsible for leaving the anchor behind in Lagos.

The second cutting—also from a UK paper—reported that following the change from driving on the left to driving on the right (which had happened a year or so earlier), all motorcycles, cars and other light vehicles would drive on the right from Sunday the 13th, and all trucks, buses and other heavy vehicles would drive on the right from the 20th.

What, exactly, was expected to happen between the 13th and the 20th?

Ghana

I flew from Lagos to Accra. At the baggage carousel I was astonished by how many sets of car tyres were coming off the aircraft. Without exaggeration, for every suitcase there were at least three sets of four tyres—tied together like drum hoops.

On the drive to my hotel—one of the best, and highly recommended, the Ambassador—it became obvious why anyone lucky enough to travel brought tyres home. Accra was full of old vehicles held together with tape and string. Almost every tyre on every car was worn down to the canvas, and many had tyres stitched over tyres to keep them on the road.

The taxi I was in wasn't quite down to canvas—but it was well past any sign of a tread pattern.

The Export Adventurer

When I reached my room, a bedroom window was wide open. On the dressing table lay a letter apologising for the lack of air conditioning due to a breakdown. Spare parts weren't available in Ghana; they were waiting for them to be imported.

The letter looked old and well handled—as though it had been sitting on that dressing table for a very long time.

Ghana, at that time, had nothing. The economy was in freefall, and there would be no market for us there for some time.

Togo

Like Ghana, Togo was very poor—around 4.5 million people, most living below the poverty line, and roughly half the population under eighteen. Where infrastructure projects existed, specifications were generally French, written by predominantly French architects, consultants and engineers.

Côte d'Ivoire

The Côte d'Ivoire Intercontinental—what a contrast. Fully air-conditioned luxury, complete with an ice rink, a tenpin bowling alley and French cordon bleu restaurants.

Unfortunately for us, as with most Francophone countries, French influence was decisive and specifications followed suit. Still, it was a splendid place to get the Lagos dust—and the aroma of Accra and Togo—out of your lungs.

The Gambia

The journey from the airport to Freetown meant crossing the very wide Gambia River. Our coach drove onto a rickety wooden floating platform, which was hauled across the 400–500-yard waterway by ropes.

As a coach or truck loaded, and cars followed on, the platform sank alarmingly low into the water.

I stayed at the British Caledonian–owned Atlantique Hotel on the expansive sands of the Gambia River. It felt odd using the restaurant dressed in smart casual while most other residents were in shorts, T-shirts and flip-flops—but someone had to do it.

I decided there was little business to be had, so I brought my flight home forward by a day. I went down to B-Cal's office in Banjul and, as I was travelling business class, getting onto the earlier flight was no problem.

As I put my tickets away, the clerk rang the hotel and told them they had to take one passenger off the flight. I felt guilty—until I returned to the hotel bar and found one happy couple celebrating. They had volunteered for their holiday to be extended at no extra cost.

When I arrived at Gatwick, I transferred by airport bus to Heathrow to catch the British Midland flight to Leeds. Looking out of the bus window, I saw uprooted trees everywhere, lying on their sides.

I asked a passenger what had happened.

It was 16 October 1987—the day after the storm that hit the UK and caused terrible damage. Michael Fish, the BBC weatherman, had assured the nation that no storm was on its way.

Sierra Leone

I arrived in Sierra Leone reading Jack Higgins' *The Dogs of War*. The main streets of Freetown looked like scenes from the book: raised wooden bungalows with verandas on all sides, topped with rusting corrugated steel.

One of the scruffiest buildings had an impressive plaque declaring it to be the British consul's office.

My market research before arriving had identified one potential player—a builders' merchant equivalent—Mr Jim Johnson. Jim was about 6'6", with a lithe, powerful build. He lived in a lovely brick-built house overlooking the river.

The Export Adventurer

One afternoon, as I took tea with Jim and his family, he suddenly began shouting at children playing in one of the river's tributaries below. Seeing my concern, he explained:

"I was telling them there were crocodiles in that creek yesterday—and to be very careful."

It's a good job we don't have crocodiles in the UK. Otherwise I'd never have let my children play out.

We did some small business together, but Sierra Leone already had local production of cast-iron and asbestos cement pipes at costs far below anything imported.

Liberia

Monrovia, Liberia, was a total waste of time—except, perhaps, for cheap ship registrations. The market had nothing to offer when I visited.

It was alleged that the president had recently been re-elected with a majority in excess of the country's total population.

Chapter 20 — Central African Republic

After West Africa, I went to Paris to negotiate a contract in the Central African Republic.

I have included the Central African Republic in this book because my involvement—brief though it was—was certainly memorable.

Jean-Bédel Bokassa proclaimed himself Emperor of the Central African Empire in 1977, staging a coronation of such extravagance that it was widely said to have emptied the treasury and consumed much of the foreign aid the country received from France. Two years later, in 1979, he was overthrown and fled the country.

In 1983, however, Bokassa returned—apparently in the belief that he might recover his crown.

It was at that point that I came into contact with the people organising what was intended to be his re-inauguration. All discussions and negotiations took place in Paris, and the Bokassa team spoke only French.

Back in the export office at Bartol, we had a colleague named Carrie. She was Dutch by origin, but spoke English and Dutch fluently, as well as French, Flemish and German. Between us, we had exactly the skills required. So, Carrie and I travelled to Paris to meet the Bokassa delegation.

The meetings ran from nine in the morning until five in the afternoon for two full days. Between Carrie's linguistic skills

The Export Adventurer

and my ability to extract quantities from drawings, we came away with a letter of intent valued at £150,000.

We were to supply all the plumbing materials for the entire project—effectively a temporary hotel complex intended to support the planned ceremony and its guests.

Carrie had never been to Paris before, so once each day's meetings ended, we did what any sensible pair of travellers would do and headed straight into the city. One evening took in Concorde, the Tuileries Garden, the Champs-Élysées and the Arc de Triomphe. The next night, Pigalle—and the Moulin Rouge.

In the end, Bokassa never regained power, and the re-inauguration never took place. The project died with it.

I understand that his son, Jean-Bédel Bokassa Jr., remains the heir apparent.

Chapter 21 — Continental Europe

Hepworth Plastics International employed a sales manager based in Paris, working jointly for Bartol Plastics, Hepworth Industrial Plastics and Fordham Plastics. His role was not to chase sales of our soil, waste and drainage systems, as these required compliance with French national standards. Instead, he focused exclusively on British Standard specifications in Africa, the Middle East and East Asia, working through European architects and consulting engineers.

With the introduction of the Acorn push-fit plumbing system, however, he began to uncover interest from distributors within Europe itself, particularly in France. In Germany, we were already selling some quantities of the Acorn PB push-fit plumbing system through Brugman Friesoplast, based in Papenburg, Friesland, in northern Germany. They had first encountered Acorn when visiting our R&D facility, following their sale to Hepworth Plastics of the technology for extruding glazing bars for the Hepworth Astra Seal double-glazing system.

I visited Brugman's CEO, Ulf Brickenstein, many times between 1982 and 1984, and we got on very well. On one occasion, he gave me a novelty gadget I still own: pressing a button fires snuff at speed up your nostrils and into your sinuses.

In the Netherlands, Belgium and France, I inherited two Acorn PB push-fit system stockists. In the Netherlands, we were represented by Martin et Cie, whose offices were in Noordwijkerhout, just north of The Hague. In Belgium, our agents were Smith Industries, based in Waterloo, south of

The Export Adventurer

Brussels. They had requested the agency after being introduced to our products through sales made to their UK branch.

I identified a shortlist of potential agents and distributors in France and eventually appointed one in Rouen. Because our agents were widely spread and often poorly served by direct air routes from the UK, most of my visits were made by car.

Travelling by car broke the mould of the international jet-setter image: early starts, airports, short flights, taxis, meetings, and the same journey repeated in reverse. That kind of travel is the bleaker side of exporting. Driving was far more effective. I could tow the company's demonstration trailer and cover Germany, Holland, Belgium and France in two or three days. Along the way, I could enjoy the countryside, experience local culture, and—crucially—save both time and money. One ferry crossing cost far less than four flights.

Occasionally, urgent matters still required flying visits, but in Western Europe these became increasingly rare.

Many of our European—and global—contacts came via exhibitions. I developed the Korean market using information gleaned from the Baghdad Fair. We also received enquiries from UK exhibitions at the NEC. One such lead took us into Sweden, following enquiries generated at the Heating and Ventilation Exhibition. One came from a company specialising in marine pumps and valves in Gothenburg; another from a manufacturer of heating systems for caravans and boats based near Trosa, about seventy kilometres south of Stockholm.

The Export Adventurer

Hooking the faithful **"Tow-a-Van"** demonstration trailer onto my company Ford Sierra Sapphire, I took the DFDS ferry from Harwich to Gothenburg. It was April, and the AA had confirmed that studded tyres were no longer required—the winter snow had supposedly gone.

I arrived in Gothenburg to bright sunshine and quickly located the prospective distributor. They had offered to arrange accommodation, which turned out to be a company apartment overlooking Gothenburg harbour. They were a good fit: the right outlook, contacts and customer base.

The next day I drove east across Sweden, from the Atlantic coast toward the Baltic. The blue sky gradually darkened, clouds thickened, and light snow began to fall—then heavier and heavier until visibility was reduced to a blinding whiteout. The road disappeared beneath packed snow. Initially, traffic kept two dark tracks open, but even those vanished.

Local drivers carried on regardless, still running winter studded tyres. I, meanwhile, was towing a trailer and praying I wouldn't have to touch the brakes. I was deeply relieved to reach the motel outside Trosa.

As soon as I stepped out of the car, disaster struck again: a tiny retaining screw had worked loose from my spectacles and one lens dropped onto the ice-crusted tarmac, shattering into pieces. I had no spare pair. That evening, I reconstructed part of the lens using superglue. By tilting my head at just the right angle, I could peer through one of the larger fragments well enough to function.

Clear vision was essential. My return journey involved driving back through Sweden, taking the ferry to Germany, then continuing through Holland, Belgium and France.

During my two-day stay in Trosa, Tommy Hyvonen, the general manager of Gastherm—the prospective agents—took me to a caravan exhibition in Stockholm. He was well known to the manufacturers; by then, virtually every caravan in Scandinavia had central heating, and Gastherm were the leading low-voltage bottled-gas boiler supplier.

Although the Stockholm pitch was impressive, Gastherm's was better. I appointed them as our Scandinavian agent for Acorn PB pipes and fittings. They soon became stockist-distributors and marketed the product successfully.

Tommy, a Finn by birth, became a close personal friend—one that endured long after both of us moved on. We often aligned our East Asian trips and met on occasions in Hong Kong, Taiwan and Korea.

He had a dry sense of humour. On one trip to Taiwan, while staying in a hotel in Kaohsiung, he complained of catching a cold.
"From what?" I asked.
"The ice," he replied.
"What ice?"
"The ice in the gin."

On another occasion, touring Sweden, we finished lunch with coffee. Tommy remarked, "Do you realise, Gerry, here we are—a Finn and a Brit—in a Chinese restaurant, in Sweden, drinking Italian coffee?"

With my head tilted back and rotated about twenty-two degrees, I could just about see enough to drive. I returned via the Trelleborg–Rostock ferry, then on to Brugman in Papenburg, Martin in Noordwijkerhout, Smith Industries in Waterloo, and finally Rouen. At each stop I stayed long enough for meaningful business discussions—and to give my neck muscles some rest. I returned home via the Le Havre–Portsmouth ferry.

Passing Doncaster on the way, I decided to drop off the demonstration trailer. Arriving at the factory at 3 a.m., I pulled up at the barrier. Nothing happened. The security guard was asleep. He was irritated when awakened and demanded, "Where the hell have you been?" My reply ended the conversation, and the barrier was raised—then promptly lowered again as I left.

On another occasion, I had just returned from a gruelling trip to Jordan, Iraq and Egypt when I arrived back in the Doncaster office on a Monday morning to find an urgent request from Smith Industries in Belgium. They needed the demonstration trailer for an exhibition. The problem was that the request had been made two weeks earlier and the exhibition was due to start later that same week.

The only way to comply was to leave immediately that evening on the North Sea Ferries service from Hull to Zeebrugge.

In those days, that meant first getting the accounts department to contact the bank in Doncaster to raise a banker's draft. That draft then had to be taken to the Sheffield Chamber of Commerce to obtain a customs ATA carnet—an

The Export Adventurer

impressively thick document containing multiple identical pages listing every single item in the "Tow-a-Van" trailer.

The carnet allowed the goods to be taken into any EEC (European Economic Community) country without paying duty, on the strict understanding that they would be removed within one year. At every border crossing, customs officials checked the carnet against the contents and removed a page for their records. Import and export pages were later reconciled. If an export page failed to appear, customs would claim the unpaid duty through the International Chamber of Commerce.

I did not relish the prospect of tearing around Doncaster and Sheffield, hitching up the trailer, packing an overnight bag and still being at St George's Dock in Hull by 6 p.m. It was 1983, the miners' strike was in full flow, and after a brief conversation with George, I decided to turn the Belgian trip into a longer circuit through Holland and Germany, returning on the Thursday from Rotterdam to Hull.

Because I was exhausted, I decided to take a friend along to share the driving—a striking miner who had time on his hands.

Charlie Boyes had been my friend since 1968, when I moved into a house three doors away from his. He worked at the local colliery but was idle due to the strike. I rang him and asked if he fancied the trip. He jumped at the chance.

After the rush of the day, we found ourselves in the ferry bar out of Hull, enjoying a well-earned drink. About an hour later, as we passed Spurn Head and exited the Humber into the North Sea, Charlie felt the gentle roll of the ship.

"It's rocking, Gerry," he said.

The Export Adventurer

"Yes," I replied, "we're in the North Sea now."

He glanced at his watch. "How long does it take to get across?"

"About fourteen hours. We're due in around eight in the morning."

The colour drained from his face.

In a subdued voice he said, "I'm not good on water. Christine said it was only ninety minutes."

I explained that ninety minutes applied to Dover–Calais, not a diagonal crossing of the North Sea. Fortunately, the crossing was calm, and after a couple of beers Charlie slept through most of it.

We arrived at Smith Industries in Waterloo at around 9:30 a.m. When André de Sauvage, the general manager, saw me pull into the car park towing the trailer, he rushed out to greet me. No one had told him I was coming.

He ran up, kissed me on both cheeks and exclaimed, in a strong Flemish accent, "Gerry, I love you!"

Charlie, a Yorkshire coal miner to the core, leaned over and whispered, "He'd better not kiss me."

We left Smith Industries by mid-morning, crossed into Holland to Noordwijkerhout to visit Martin et Cie, and then continued on to Amsterdam, where we stayed at the Sonesta Hotel.

That evening, during a walk through the nearby red-light district, we noticed a pale green canal-side building with large white plaster reliefs on the façade. A short flight of steps led

The Export Adventurer

up to a raised green door. People climbed the steps, knocked, were viewed through a peephole, and admitted.

Curious, we tried our luck and were welcomed in.

Inside, a receptionist explained that this was a "religious order" and that payment was required in advance. A quick calculation showed it worked out at roughly one pound per minute. I decided to invest £60—thirty minutes each—to find out what was going on. It was stressed that overstaying was not appreciated.

Inside, it looked like a conventional bar, moderately busy, with roughly equal numbers of men and women. The difference was the bar itself: instead of a recess behind it, several naked young women served drinks while moving on hands and knees across a fully padded bar top.

We sat on two empty stools. I ordered a gin and tonic; Charlie stuck to beer.

From time to time, a man would turn away from the bar, lay his head back onto the padded surface and place a folded ten-guilder note on his nose. One of the women would remove it—without using her hands.

Cheering erupted from another room. We went to investigate.

Four performers were surrounded by a ring of about thirty holidaymakers, mostly aged between eighteen and thirty. One performer moved around the ring, instructing men to stand with legs apart and bend forward. She then lay on her back, lifted her hips, and fired a vibrator toward their faces. Missed catches resulted in the device being rinsed in their beer before another attempt. Each man got three tries.

The Export Adventurer

Another performer smoked a cigar clenched internally. Another crushed ping-pong balls using pelvic muscles. Yet another accepted neckties, fed them inside herself, and slowly returned them to their owners. The final performer sold personalised postcards.

Audience participation was enthusiastic, particularly from the women.

We left exactly on time. Outside, I remarked to Charlie, "I bet you can't wait to tell your mates about that."

He replied dryly, "What—that I spent thirty quid to watch some **** smoke?"

After a few Amstel beers elsewhere, we turned in early. We needed a very early start if we were to reach Papenburg in time for an afternoon meeting.

The next morning, just before seven, I was walking toward the lift when I encountered a flustered Charlie and an elderly woman shouting from her room in thick German-accented English, "How dare you call me a Jerry!"

Charlie later confessed he had knocked on the wrong door, announcing loudly, "Come on, Gerry, time to get up."

No wonder she was unimpressed.

We drove north via Groningen and arrived in Papenburg in good time. Ulf Brickenstein was delighted to see us and insisted on taking us out to dinner. He explained he could only stay until about eight because he had another engagement.

The Export Adventurer

He took us to a luxurious bar-cum-brothel halfway toward Bremen. Draped ceilings, plush couches, oak tables, and stunning hostesses in sheer negligees completed the scene.

Ulf stayed for one drink, then explained he had instructed the barman to arrange a taxi for us when we wished to leave.

After he departed, two young women joined us. I struggled through half an hour of schoolboy German, while overhearing Charlie's conversation next to me. His companion was trying hard to persuade him into a private room.

"Just tell me what number you want," she said.

"I couldn't even paint by numbers," Charlie replied, "never mind make love to them."

She didn't understand. I did.

Eventually, I realised my companion was explaining—at length—that she had recently crashed her car into a tree. When I finally asked, in English, "Where are you from?" she replied, "Huddersfield."

Enough was enough.

When I asked for a taxi, the barman queried why we were leaving so early. I explained we had an early start and limited Deutschmarks. He informed us that Ulf had left instructions for anything we wanted to be charged to his account. A generous gesture—but we'd had quite enough.

The next day, at Ulf's request, we drove to Hamburg to visit one of his clients, leaving Papenburg at 7 a.m. We checked into the Berlin Hotel before lunch.

The Export Adventurer

After a two-hour meeting, we spent the evening on the Reeperbahn: steak, apple strudel, bars, bordellos, and another live sex show—cheap beer included. The performers used a signalling system: when a tout looked close to recruiting customers, a flashlight cue sent the performers into high energy. Thirty seconds later, enthusiasm waned again.

I visited Europe constantly between 1981 and 1984—sometimes by air, mostly by car. The number of ferry crossings I used says everything:

Hull–Rotterdam
Hull–Zeebrugge
Zeebrugge–Dover
Barcelona–Palma
Harwich–Esbjerg
Harwich–Gothenburg
Helsingør–Helsingborg
Rostock–Trelleborg
Dover–Calais
Dover–Dunkirk
Dover–Boulogne
Folkestone–Calais
Folkestone–Dunkirk
Folkestone–Boulogne
Portsmouth–Caen
Portsmouth–St Malo
Portsmouth–Cherbourg
Portsmouth–Le Havre
Southampton–Le Havre
Liverpool–Dublin
Holyhead–Dún Laoghaire
Holyhead–Dublin
Larne–Stranraer
Nyborg–Korsør
Kavala–Thasos

The Export Adventurer

One January, George Bell and I travelled to Brussels, Paris and Rouen during severe cold. When I collected him in Rotherham, he was carrying a huge bottle of washing-up liquid. He explained it might help if the washer jets froze.

They did—somewhere on the French autoroute in freezing fog. George wound down the window, reached out, and squirted detergent onto the windscreen. It worked—briefly. Then the spray froze onto his arm, turning his shirt sleeve into a rigid ice cast.

The next day, heading toward Rouen, George reclined in the passenger seat and fell asleep with his stockinged feet on the dashboard. Fifty kilometres later, we were stopped by police who had seen "two feet where the driver's head should have been" travelling slightly above 130 kph.

We paid the fine in cash. At lunch in Rouen, our agent's CEO quietly examined the paperwork, left the room, and thirty minutes later the police officer arrived and refunded the fine. Connections matter.

All this European travel ran alongside frequent trips to the Caribbean, Middle East, Far East and Australasia. I was rarely at home—but I was enjoying myself enormously.

Cyprus

I only ever visited Cyprus once on business, which was at the request of our colleagues at Fordham Plastics, whose agent had asked for assistance with a project involving some plastic drainage. I combined the trip with one to Lebanon and arrived from Beirut.

I stayed at the rather swish five-star Churchill hotel in Limassol. The hotel overlooked the beach, and the Fordham plastics agent collected and returned me to the hotel each day. He was a charming chap who wanted to add the Bartol agency to his portfolio of products. Our products were complementary to Fordham's and supplied to the same clientele. So, the decision to appoint him was not a difficult one.

He took me out, and we had the most delicious Mezza, which concluded with the most delightful pork (suckling pig) I have ever tasted.

I cannot recall why but I needed to visit the British Embassy, which I found was behind the Turkish partition lines, and the road to the embassy from the Greek side was picked out in oil drums. It was a bizarre experience driving between two lines of oil drums where the jurisdictional authority on both sides differed from that on the road.

It was a petrol heads paradise, with immaculate classic British cars in daily use. The dry climate had preserved so many classic cars that they were a pleasure to behold.

It would be 35 years before I revisited Cyprus.

Malta

Malta was another market where enquiries led to the visit, and I recall arriving on Alitalia from Rome. I stayed in the Sliema Hilton.

My long-lasting impression of Malta was that the Knights of St George had done such an excellent job with the battlements that, in most places, the easiest way onto many beaches was by parachute.

Chapter 22 — Ireland

Southern Ireland had historically been serviced from a stock point in Northern Ireland. Home sales, however, found Ireland impossible to deal with. They traded only in sterling yet frequently received payment in Irish punts against sterling invoices, which resulted in us being consistently underpaid by around twenty per cent.

When I received the sales records for Southern Ireland, I was alarmed to discover that we were owed close to £100,000—and that no representative had visited our customers for almost three months. If we were going to retain the loyalty of Builders' Providers, as builders' merchants are known in Ireland, we had to ensure they did not feel compelled to look elsewhere for supplies.

Armed with lists of everyone who owed us money, I set off on a one-week discovery tour of Southern Ireland. I began in Dublin and headed south down the east coast to Waterford and Cork, then on to Kenmare on the Ring of Kerry, before working my way back up the west coast via Limerick and Galway, finally reaching Letterkenny in Donegal. I visited every Builders' Provider on the route.

What I discovered was both alarming and reassuring. The only reason we had received no orders for three months was simply that no representative had called to collect them. Furthermore, payment for previous supplies had not been made because it was traditional for the representative to collect payment at the same time as the next order. Bartol Plastics—not the customers—had broken the cycle.

I converted all outstanding sterling invoices into punts and had no difficulty whatsoever collecting the full amounts owed.

The Export Adventurer

Mike Marsden discovered I was in Ireland on the Wednesday of that week and phoned me early in the morning at my hotel. He was concerned that I might be setting up something new in Ireland that could complicate debt collection. He backed off rapidly when I told him I had already recovered eighty per cent of the outstanding balance.

Over the following months, I made four further trips to Southern Ireland. I ran exhibitions of the Acorn PB push-fit plumbing system in Cork, Limerick, and Letterkenny.

At the time, I was still driving my original 1600cc powder-blue Ford Escort—exactly the same colour as Garda police cars. On my second visit, I was leaving the docks in Dublin, uncertain of the route, when sirens sounded and blue lights appeared behind me. I pulled over.

The Garda officer said, "I noticed you weren't wearing your seatbelt, sir."

"I'm very sorry," I replied. "I didn't know it was a legal requirement in Ireland."

"Oh," he said cheerfully, "it's not—but it is much safer if you wear it."

I never did work out if that was truly the reason he stopped me.

On another occasion, I was leaving Kenmare at about five in the morning, driving back to Dublin to catch the lunchtime ferry to Liverpool. The first twenty miles were narrow country lanes. As I rounded a Z-bend and crossed a humpbacked bridge, two Garda officers were standing in the middle of the road, one holding a clipboard.

The Export Adventurer

"Can you tell us where you're going?" one asked.

"To Dublin."

"And where are you from?"

"Kenmare."

"No," he said patiently, "where are you really from?"

"England."

At that, the officer with the clipboard sighed with visible relief and said, "Ah—that explains the registration number then."

To this day, I wonder what they were looking for.

In Cork, I met a young ex-plumber in his early thirties who was importing and distributing Swiss radiator valves. He was enthusiastic about the Acorn PB push-fit system, and it was an ideal fit for us to appoint him as our commission agent. He already visited all our potential customers and knew the plumbing trade inside out.

Approval of potable water systems in Ireland depended heavily on minimum flow rates. Because Acorn PB pipe had a thicker wall than equivalent 15 mm copper pipe, its internal bore was slightly smaller, and the approving authority was reluctant to sanction it.

I pointed out that most plumbers cut copper pipe using wheeled cutting tools, which invariably roll the cut end inward, restricting flow. Our system, properly installed, maintained a larger continuous bore than traditional copper. After reconsideration, the authority approved the product.

The Export Adventurer

Over the next two years, I visited Ireland three or four times annually. On one occasion, I brought the demonstration trailer with me, running exhibitions at Elms Builders' Providers in Cork and later in Letterkenny for our local stockist, Jim Johnson. After the evening demonstration at Jim's premises, we went back to his house for dinner. I left shortly after midnight to catch the three-a.m. ferry from Larne.

The Troubles were still ongoing, and the route took me through Londonderry. Jim advised me that if anyone stopped me and demanded the car, I should get out and walk away without resistance. The approach to the border was zigzagged, and the buildings resembled reinforced concrete military bunkers, fortified with sandbags.

As I approached the barrier slowly, a hand holding a torch appeared from the side of one of the buildings and waved me through. The barrier lifted. I saw nothing more than a torch and a wrist.

One of my favourite calls was McSweeney's in Galway. Dermot always insisted I take a bottle of poitín—undiluted whiskey straight from the still. Taken neat, it was strong enough to anaesthetise your lips. On one occasion, a customs officer in Liverpool found a bottle hidden inside my Wellington boot. He told me I could have been jailed if caught with poitín in Ireland.

I asked what the penalty was in England.

"Here," he said, "it's a bottle of whisky—and you're allowed one."

Sales in Southern Ireland of the Acorn push-fit plumbing system, along with our traditional soil, waste, and drainage products, flourished under our agent's care.

Chapter 23 — Australia

Australasia first popped onto the agenda in 1983 when a senior employee from New Zealand's Mico Wakefield Group visited us in Doncaster.

Up to that point we'd done no real research in either Australia or New Zealand. Even so, Australia had been in the back of my mind for two reasons. First, I knew Yorkshire Imperial Metals had a clone operation—Yorkshire Imperial Australia—based around Sydney. Second, two of my brothers had emigrated there in the early 1970s. I'd seen my older brother, Laurie, because he'd visited the UK a couple of times, but I hadn't seen Steve—my closest sibling, only eighteen months older than me—since he left.

I was due to fly out to Kuala Lumpur around then, so I asked our travel agent what it would cost to add Sydney and Auckland onto the itinerary. To my surprise, flying to Sydney via Kuala Lumpur—or to Auckland via Kuala Lumpur—on Malaysian Airline System was cheaper than flying to Kuala Lumpur alone.

The only explanation was heavy discounting to compete with BA, Qantas and Air New Zealand on those long-haul routes. Either way, it was a useful discovery. Every time I went to East Asia, I could tack on Australia or New Zealand and actually *save* Bartol money—savings I was more than happy to deliver, repeatedly.

On my first business trip to Australia, I phoned Steve from Kuala Lumpur to warn him I was coming. I was leaving KL for Bangkok the following day, spending an afternoon and night there, then flying on Royal Thai to Sydney.

The Export Adventurer

When we landed at Kingsford Smith, the aircraft was parked out on the apron some distance from the terminal. A team in white protective clothing and goggles boarded and sprayed the entire cabin with insecticide. The passengers, of course, were offered no protection whatsoever.

Immigration moved slowly. The official—summer uniform, shorts—subjected each passenger to a fairly thorough inspection and interrogation before waving them into the customs hall. When it was my turn, he immediately clocked my birthplace: Tadcaster. By sheer chance, he'd done his national service with the RAF at Church Fenton.

His manner changed instantly. We spent the next five minutes chatting about what had changed in the area—which was very little. Church Fenton was still operational, and the villages looked much as they had when I was an infant.

Steve was waiting when I finally emerged into the terminal. It was as though we'd never been apart; seven missing years simply evaporated.

Although I was staying with him in Sydney, I hired a car because I needed to move around meeting potential agents, distributors and—ideally—licensees. Steve had leased a Caltex petrol station and garage in Forestville and lived nearby in St Ives, both in Sydney's northern suburbs.

I spent a week in Sydney, working during the day and catching up in the evenings and at weekends. I found two possible partners who might have helped us develop the market, but nothing that truly leapt off the page.

During the years I was based in Kuala Lumpur and then Korea for Bartol–Hepworth, I used the family-status air tickets built into my contract to take the whole family on holidays together—Malaysia, Hong Kong, Korea and Australia.

On one trip, my family flew out to KL and joined me for a few days. We visited Penang, then continued on to Sydney for a few weeks. About an hour out from Sydney the aircraft was struck by lightning—fortunately with no damage beyond a brief collective silence in the cabin.

Steve later bought a farm about seventy kilometres north of Sydney in the Dooralong Valley, and we holidayed there. My teenage children loved the horses and driving tractors—until one incident very nearly turned tragic.

My daughter, Jayne, was bitten by a funnel-web spider. We rushed her towards the nearest hospital in Wyong while an ambulance carrying the antivenom raced towards us. We met on the road and the antidote was administered there and then. Jayne remained ill for a few days, but she recovered quickly and returned to her usual self.

Australia is a wonderful place to be if you have a reasonably developed sense of humour, because Australians love to laugh—especially at themselves. I was once booked on a flight from Melbourne to Sydney on Trans-Australian Airways, not long after they'd shortened their name to "Australian". The captain's welcome ran:

The Export Adventurer

"Good morning, ladies and gentlemen, welcome aboard this Trans-Australian Airways—shit—*AUSTRALIAN* flight to Sydney..."

On another flight—Central Coast to Sydney—the stewardess, while demonstrating the lifejacket, advised everyone not to use the whistle because it would "attract the sharks".

On a later visit, I was in the Dooralong cricket club having a drink with Steve and a few locals when the conversation turned to the traditional sport of ribbing the pommy in the room. So, I asked each of them when they—or their families—had arrived in Oz. One claimed fourth-generation Australian, another second-generation. Steve was seven years in. Two others said twenty and thirty years respectively.

I pointed out that to be second or fourth generation, the original family members were quite likely transported prisoners of Mother England—POMEs—and the rest had taken advantage of the famous £10 assisted passage scheme.

Which meant I was the only one in the room fully entitled to be there—because I'd paid my own full fare.

I only visited Melbourne once, but it was an absolute delight. The city—with its trams and cobbled lanes—reminded me of Zürich. Shell Australia, who were hosting me, put me into the most sumptuous hotel I'd stayed in up to that point: the Menzies at Rialto—two converted old mill buildings joined under a glass roof over a cobbled courtyard. The rooms and service were impeccable.

My hosts gave me a city tour. We visited bars serving every variety of Australian amber nectar, and one even stocked Newcastle Brown.

It felt like a privilege to be there on business.

From Australia, attention shifted naturally across the Tasman, where a very different market presented itself.

Chapter 24 — Nrw Zealand

On my first visit, I started in Auckland, where I had one or two appointments. However, the most memorable meeting was with Shell New Zealand, who took me to lunch in the revolving restaurant on top of the Sky Tower. They explained how polybutylene (PB) had taken the New Zealand market by storm. It was the only flexible plastic material available that could reliably handle the high temperatures encountered there.

In the UK, building regulations at that time limited the temperature of domestic water and central-heating systems to a maximum of 82°C. In New Zealand, however, water was often heated by underground thermal activity, and temperatures were frequently well above that limit. There were already two companies extruding polybutylene pipes, and I added these manufacturers to the list of calls I had already planned.

Virtually none of the manufacturers were based in Auckland, so my next stop was Wellington. Almost everyone I met was desperate to obtain the manufacturing rights to the Acorn system. Australian and New Zealand pipe dimensions were still imperial, so any prospect of supplying product from the United Kingdom was a non-starter.

The most interesting visit—before my final meeting with the Mico Wakefield Group—was to one of the companies suggested by our contacts at Shell. Buteline was run by a chap from the East End of London, Dave Picton. Dave was already using the same brown Shell 4139 resin that we used in the UK. That surprised me, because Bartol Plastics was under the impression that it held worldwide exclusivity on that particular resin.

The Export Adventurer

Buteline were using the American system of crimping the pipe onto acetyl fittings. Acetyl fittings ran into major problems in the 1990s in the United States, when the material became brittle as chlorine was added to water supplies. I understand that the modern Buteline system no longer uses acetyl fittings.

Looking back, cooperation between Hepworth and Buteline could have been a marriage made in heaven, with PB pipe and PB fittings. However, acetyl had yet to fail, and Dave was not interested in purchasing any technology from us at that stage.

I concluded that Mico Wakefield—who had almost a plumbers' merchant in every large town on both the North and South Islands, and who were prepared to invest in setting up a PB pipe and fittings factory from scratch—would be the ideal partner in New Zealand.

They convened a meeting of their senior people: the general manager of their extrusion plant, members of their sales teams, directors, and the elderly chairman, Ziggy Hirschfeld, together with his CEO son, David.

There were about twenty people around the boardroom table. We went through the many advantages and disadvantages of push-fit PB pipes and fittings. One of the sales managers—probably trying to impress the directors—asked, "Mr Bratley, what can we do about the licence down payment?"

I replied, "I could put it up."

David Hirschfield intervened immediately and said, "We have already agreed to US$50,000. Let us leave it at that."

The Export Adventurer

Six weeks later, David Hirschfield travelled to London, and I met him at the Tower Hotel, where we signed the licensing agreement.

A few weeks after that, I returned to New Zealand to begin handing over the technical information. David Slater, the extrusion-plant general manager, commented that he had been racking his brain for months trying to work out how a relatively complex thermoplastic could be extruded with such consistently tight manufacturing tolerances. Now that they had the licence, I was able to divulge the information about the die-head pump.

He spent the next thirty minutes remonstrating with himself for not having reached that conclusion on his own.

When I was leaving New Zealand, I was booked on Pan Am from Auckland to Sydney. Pan Am ceased trading, but fortunately Qantas stepped in, took over all Pan Am's Pacific routes, and honoured the ticket.

Business Class upstairs on that Qantas Boeing 747 had sheepskin-covered seats, and the flight attendants addressed you by name. After the pre-take-off drinks, they prepared a meal and were about to serve it.

The stewardess approached me and asked, "Mr Bratley, would you like some caviar?"

I replied, "That would be very nice," as I like anything fishy.

She then turned to the gentleman beside me and asked if he would like some caviar. He asked what it was.

"It's fish's eggs, sir," she replied.

The Export Adventurer

"I'll have two boiled," he said.

I left the employment of Bartol–Hepworth before the plant in New Zealand produced any product.

Chapter 25 — Japan

In 1981, we received a request from Kubota in Osaka, Japan, enquiring about the possibility of manufacturing the Acorn PB pipes and fittings locally.

Mount Fuji taken from BA005

Instead of taking my routine flight from London to Korea via Hong Kong, our travel agent routed me over the North Pole on British Airways flight BA 005. In those days, the flight stopped in Anchorage for refuelling before continuing down the Aleutian Islands to Tokyo and then on to Osaka. It was the first time I had crossed the International Date Line.

The devastation from the Mount St Helens eruption in October 1980 was still clearly visible from the air. Many square miles of charred tree stumps lay flattened on the ground, all pointing in the same direction—a stark reminder of the scale of the blast.

Anchorage airport itself had a striking exhibit: a stuffed polar bear in a glass case, rearing up on its hind legs to a height of around ten feet. It was an arresting sight, and not particularly reassuring.

The Export Adventurer

In Osaka, I was met at the airport by a bowing chauffeur holding a card with my name on it. He insisted on wheeling my luggage trolley himself and led me to a substantial black Toyota limousine—a model I had never seen outside Japan. He handed me an envelope and drove me directly to the hotel Kubota had booked for me.

Inside the envelope was a welcoming note along with a copy of the itinerary they had prepared. I was due to be collected in three hours for dinner.

On arrival at the hotel, two bellboys bowed and took my luggage from the driver. As I entered through the front door, two young women opened each of the double doors and bowed. I passed the concierge, who bowed, then the receptionist, who bowed again.

After checking in, I walked towards the lifts. Two more young women in national dress stood on either side of the lift doors; both bowed and pressed the call button for me. When the lift arrived, the lift operator bowed as I entered, and bowed again as I exited on my floor.

On the landing, two further young women stood on either side of the lift doors and bowed as I walked out.

I have to say that being shown such constant and formal respect made me feel uncomfortable—and completely unworthy of it.

In the safe sanctuary of my room, I finally felt able to relax. I called room service and ordered some coffee. Shortly afterwards, the doorbell rang. Two bellboys arrived with my luggage, bowed when they entered, bowed again when they left, and bowed once more when the coffee was delivered by the waiter.

The Export Adventurer

I had a leisurely two-hour rest, showered, and got ready for the dinner appointment. Precisely at the appointed time, the telephone rang. My hosts were waiting in reception.

As I left my room, the girls at the lift bowed and pressed the call button. The lift operator bowed. On reaching the ground floor, the two attendants bowed again. In the foyer, which was full of Japanese guests, three people noticed the rare appearance of a European and approached me politely to confirm my identity. I held out my hand; they bowed.

As we left the hotel, the concierge, door attendants, and hotel porters all bowed. I remember thinking how dreadful it would have been to realise I had forgotten something and needed to go back upstairs.

My three hosts were unfailingly courteous and explained that the evening was purely social; all business discussions would be left until we were in their offices the following day.

Dinner was excellent: a superb steak accompanied by tempura vegetables—thin slices of zucchini, onion, aubergine, carrot, bell pepper, and sweet potato—deep-fried in an exceptionally light batter, all washed down with sake.

The following day, when I arrived once more in the Kubota limousine at their plant, I noticed that the Union Jack was flying alongside the Japanese flag above the headquarters building—a thoughtful and impressive gesture.

The reception area was within a large demonstration hall displaying a vast range of Kubota products, from tiny plastic components to enormous Terex-style dump trucks. Almost every farm in East Asia seems to have a ride-on Kubota rotavator or plough.

One product that particularly caught my attention was a memory-controlled lawnmower. According to the instructions, you placed the mower on the lawn, marked its starting position with four studs, pressed a memory-record button, and mowed the lawn. Thereafter, whenever the grass needed cutting, you simply positioned the mower over the same studs and left it to get on with the job.

I visited Kubota three times over the following eighteen months. Although we held very detailed and serious discussions, the negotiations never progressed to licensed local production.

Osaka now has Kansai International Airport, built on an artificial island in the bay. Back in the 1980s, however, it was still the old Osaka airport, where aircraft had to land and take off extremely low over the elevated highway serving the terminal—an experience that was memorable in its own right.

Chapter 26 — United States

I only ever made one business visit to the United States, although I passed through it many times on my way to and from other markets.

After discovering that the brown Shell 4139 polybutylene resin we used was already being supplied to manufacturers in New Zealand—a resin on which Bartol-Hepworth UK believed it had exclusivity—I decided to call on Shell Chemicals in Houston on my next trip to East Asia.

Shell booked me into a super-deluxe hotel, as one might expect in downtown Houston. My appointment was at 9 a.m. the following morning, so I went out to familiarise myself with the location. The hotel was diagonally opposite the Shell building, separated by a crossroads with four lanes of traffic running in each direction. The junction was equipped with pedestrian "Walk Now" lights, so I went to bed content, knowing exactly where I had to go.

The next morning, I had breakfast and set off at 8:50 a.m. to walk the 200 metres or so to the Shell building. As soon as I stepped outside, the July Texas sun hit me like a wall. The contrast between the hotel's air-conditioned interior and the dry, arid heat of a Houston summer was startling. Although I was used to the Middle East's desert heat and the Far East's wet heat, this was something else entirely—especially as I was wearing a business suit and tie.

As I approached the junction, I noticed something odd. At rush hour, I was the only pedestrian on the streets. The walk itself was uneventful, but when I entered the Shell building foyer, it was packed with people arriving and leaving via the lifts.

The Export Adventurer

I mentioned this strange absence of pedestrians to my hosts, who explained that downtown Houston was criss-crossed by air-conditioned underground walkways connecting offices, hotels, and transport hubs. Everyone used them to avoid both the heat and the traffic.

My meetings with Shell went well, and they were exemplary hosts. One evening they took me to dinner on the seafront at Galveston Bay, where we enjoyed the local speciality of soft-shell crab. On another night, they took me out of the city to a lively Wild West–style bar called Hog's Breath.

From Houston, I flew via Dallas–Fort Worth to Seattle, and then onward on Northwest Orient Airlines to Osaka for another meeting with Kubota.

I passed through the United States on two further occasions, linking East Asian and Australasian trips with the Caribbean.

On one occasion, I left Sydney on Friday the 13th, fully expecting to lose the unlucky day at the International Date Line. I got it wrong. According to my watch, I arrived in San Francisco on Friday the 13th—two hours before I had taken off.

I was booked into the Mark Hopkins Inter-Continental Hotel at the wonderfully improbable address of One Nob Hill. By that stage of the trip, I had already visited Japan, Korea, Taiwan, Hong Kong, Malaysia, Singapore, and Australia. I also had an overnight stay booked in Miami before flying on to meet Charles Hammerson for a full sweep of the Leeward and Windward Islands in the Caribbean. It was the longest trip I ever undertook—seven weeks in total.

I frequently stayed in Inter-Continental hotels and held one of their Six Continents Club frequent guest cards. At the Mark

The Export Adventurer

Hopkins, there was a dedicated check-in desk for Six Continents members. The receptionist introduced herself as Finlandia. She informed me that, as a club member, I was entitled to a complimentary bottle of Californian red or white wine—or champagne.

I told her I had already enjoyed plenty of Californian red and white and would be delighted to try the champagne.

A few minutes after I reached my room, there was a knock at the door. Two room-service waiters arrived pushing a large stainless-steel bucket on a trolley. Inside was a magnum of champagne.

I made the most of the unexpected two-day weekend break. I walked the city's famous zig-zag streets, rode the cable cars, took a helicopter flight from Pier 39 around Alcatraz and under the Golden Gate Bridge, and had dinner at Fisherman's Wharf.

On the flight to Miami, on a bright, cloudless day, the aircraft flew out over Death Valley, across the Las Vegas Strip, along the full length of the Grand Canyon, and then over the Barringer Meteor Crater in Arizona—three-quarters of a mile in diameter. It felt as though American Airlines were giving me a guided sightseeing tour.

The Export Adventurer

On another occasion, I flew to East Asia via the Middle East, Korea, and Japan, and then onward to Barbados via New Orleans. I spent a few days at the Hilton on Wilshire Boulevard in Los Angeles, touring the city and Hollywood. Unfortunately, my time in New Orleans was limited to a few hours, and I never left the airport.

These two trips, together with an earlier one that included flying from London via Anchorage to Japan, were the three occasions on which I set off in one direction and arrived home from the other—having circumnavigated the globe.

Chapter 27 — Hong Kong

I first travelled to Hong Kong in the spring of 1982 on my way to Taiwan and South Korea. In those days, the Chinese would not allow any flights to cross from the Soviet Union into Chinese airspace and, conversely, the Russians would not allow flights from China into Soviet airspace. These restrictions meant that from London, Korea and Japan could be reached by one of three routes:

1. Over the polar route via Greenland, the North Pole and Anchorage, which was the BA and Japan Airlines route
2. Over Russian Siberia and out onto the Pacific over Vladivostok, which was the KLM route
3. Via Bahrain and Hong Kong, which was the Cathay Pacific route

At that time, BA did not provide a service to Seoul.

The approach to Hong Kong's Kai Tak Airport, located on the west side of Kowloon Bay, was either a very spectacular event or relatively gentle, depending entirely on which way the wind was blowing when the aircraft was landing.

If the wind was blowing off the land out into the South China Sea, the approach—other than the mountains on Hong Kong Island—was largely unobstructed, coming in from seaward. However, if the wind was blowing off the South China Sea onto the land, the approach to Kai Tak was much more precarious. The airport was surrounded by rugged mountains rising to around 2,000 feet to the north and northeast of the runway. At the landward end of the runway were the six-storey buildings and apartments of Kowloon. At around 500 feet, just above a major multi-lane arterial road, the aircraft had to make

The Export Adventurer

a 45-degree turn and then drop onto the runway. Victoria Harbour surrounded the other three sides.

The low-altitude turn immediately before the shortened final approach was so spectacular inside the aircraft that washing lines and television aerials flashed past the windows so close you could see television sets glowing inside the apartments.

The runway itself had been constructed by reclaiming land from the harbour and had been extended several times to cope with ever-increasing aircraft size. By 1982, with the introduction of wide-bodied 747s, DC-10s, TriStars and Airbuses, the aircraft were again outgrowing the runway's length. One or two incidents occurred where aircraft finished their landing with more than just a nose wheel in the sea.

My first landing in Hong Kong was a particularly dramatic one. As the wheels touched the tarmac directly in front of the terminal buildings, reverse thrust and brakes were applied with such vigour that you would have been thrown forward had your seatbelt not restrained you.

It was surreal looking out at the narrow grass strip between the runway and the sea, with Chinese junks and modern freighters sailing past only yards away.

The aircraft slowed to taxiing speed and then turned immediately left, only a few yards from the water, to taxi back to the terminal at the opposite end of the runway. It was very early morning, and as we taxied back, we passed a British naval warship in the harbour with its entire crew on deck, piping up the Union Jack.

It was my very first arrival in Hong Kong. I would go on to make around seventy visits in the years that followed. One detail I still recall clearly is that the terminal buildings all had non-slip, studded tiled floors that produced a distinctive vibrating noise as wheeled trolleys and suitcases were pulled across them.

We already had a contact in Hong Kong—Paul Au Engineers—who had an office in the Central District on Hong Kong Island, opposite the Macau Ferry Terminal, overlooking Victoria Harbour.

On that first morning, I arrived at my hotel before 9 a.m. After the 17-hour flight via Bahrain, I felt slightly disorientated because it was still only 1 a.m. in the UK. With the excitement of being in Hong Kong for the first time and a mid-morning appointment with Paul Au, I opted for a walk along Nathan Road. Within thirty minutes, I had been seduced by the glittering shop windows and duty-free prices and returned to my hotel armed with a brand-new Olympus OM-10 camera.

On that first visit, I stayed at the Hyatt Regency on Nathan Road in Kowloon. It was a five-minute walk to the Star Ferry terminal, a seven-pence, five-minute crossing on the first-class upper deck, followed by another five-minute walk to Paul Au's office.

Paul took me out to lunch on one of the ladder streets just a short walk from his office. These are steep streets running up the slopes towards the Peak, built exclusively for foot traffic, with steps all the way.

The Export Adventurer

It was an older part of town, full of traditional restaurants serving traditional food. Paul ordered, and I ate. We started with delicious savoury dim sum dumplings, and then I was surprised when the next course arrived: a huge ball of baked clay on a silver salver, placed directly in front of me along with a small brass hammer.

I looked quizzically at Paul, who explained that the hammer was to break the clay. One strike shattered it. The staff removed the salver to a trolley, peeled away the clay, and revealed a chicken that had been baked unplucked. As the clay came away, it removed the feathers and skin, leaving a perfectly cooked, juicy chicken—complete with head and feet.

The salver was placed on the lazy Susan in the centre of the table, releasing a mouth-watering aroma. It was perfect, except for one thing: the head, eyes intact, was staring straight at me. Paul explained that pauper's chicken was a traditional dish designed to be cooked on an open fire without pots or utensils. As he spoke, I casually rotated the lazy Susan so that the chicken was looking elsewhere.

After lychees and cream, the final course was a vegetable soup—typical Chinese dining logic—ending with a liquefied dish to cleanse the palate. The soup consisted of shredded herbs and vegetables in a thin consommé, with a few chickpeas and kidney beans.

When I bit into one of the kidney beans, it had such a strange taste that my imagination went into overdrive. I convinced myself that the kidney bean had actually been the body of a cockroach. Feeling instantly nauseous, I examined the rest of the soup; every shred of vegetable now resembled antennae or spiky legs. I ate no more.

The Export Adventurer

I crammed as much as possible into that first visit. Once the business was concluded, I booked a half-day tour of Hong Kong Island: Aberdeen and the floating population, Stanley Market, Tiger Balm Gardens, the Peak viewing platform, and the stepped streets of Central.

I rode the trams, took the Peak Tram, and thoroughly enjoyed the day. The following day was Sunday, so I booked a tour of Kowloon and the New Territories. We were shown the twin 36-inch GRP pipes supplying fresh water to Hong Kong from China, and I was astonished by the number of duck farms scattered throughout the New Territories.

Every time I visited Hong Kong, Paul Au took me to a different kind of restaurant. Some specialised exclusively in dim sum dumplings. These restaurants operate quite differently: there are no menus. You are seated, and as dishes are prepared, they are wheeled around in stacked bamboo steamers. If you like the look of something, you take a basket, and the waitress marks it on a tally sheet at your table.

The Export Adventurer

There are dumplings filled with seafood, beef, duck, chicken, mince—every conceivable savoury and sweet filling imaginable. Everything is freshly cooked and delivered directly from the kitchen, making the quality exceptional. At the end of the meal, the tally is added up to produce the bill.

One particularly amusing incident involved the injection-moulding expert from Korea. He hated kimchi and found its smell unbearable. At the end of his visit, he was returning to the UK via Hong Kong on Cathay Pacific, and I needed to visit Kuala Lumpur, so I joined him on the Seoul–Hong Kong leg. We both had to stay overnight, and I booked us into the Hyatt Regency.

It was near Jimmy's Kitchen, where I planned to treat him to traditional English food. Unfortunately, it was already 11 p.m. when we arrived, so we decided to have lunch there the following day instead.

We were given adjoining rooms. Mike asked for food as soon as we arrived. I told him to order whatever he wanted from room service while I showered.

When I emerged fifteen minutes later, Mike appeared at my door looking ghostly pale and gasped, "They only have a snake."

I pointed to the 24-hour room-service menu and said, "You can have almost anything."

The Export Adventurer

He insisted, "I phoned them. They said they only have a snake."

I picked up the phone, asked him what he wanted—sirloin steak and chips—and called room service. The response was immediate: "I am sorry, sir, we only have snake."

Trying to stay calm, I asked, "What kind of snake?"

The reply came: "Hamburger, club sandwich, BLT sandwich, lasagne, chips—snacks, sir."

They meant *snacks*, not *snakes*. The only thing unavailable was the steak, which was on the daytime menu.

Mike had a burger and chips; I had a club sandwich and chips with coffee.

The next day, Mike began losing his balance and pirouetting on the pavement. A doctor diagnosed an ear infection, meaning we had to remain in Hong Kong for three extra days until the antibiotics worked and he was fit to endure the 17-hour pressurised flight home.

When I returned to the UK, the Bartol comedians suggested I had given Mike hearing AIDS.

As a self-confessed foodie, East Asia was—and still is—my dream destination. I love century eggs: fresh eggs preserved in their shells until the white turns into a smoky translucent jelly and the yolk solidifies into black. They look utterly inedible but taste just like hard-boiled eggs.

Chinese restaurants in Asia are not like those in the UK. There are no generic "Chinese" restaurants—only Cantonese, Fujian, Mongolian, Sichuan and other provincial cuisines, each specialising exclusively in its own food. Only in recent years have hotel banquets begun offering pan-Chinese menus to satisfy tourists. To experience real Chinese food, you must eat regionally.

On my final visit to Hong Kong in 2017, I was disappointed to find that the Jumbo Floating Restaurant in Aberdeen Harbour was no longer operating. It had always been a favourite—choosing live seafood from tanks after a boat ride past the floating communities. Since the handover to China, the boat people have vanished.

Sales to Hong Kong were never particularly strong. Most came through Crown Agents in London supplying British military installations. One UK competitor already manufactured pipes and fittings locally, so aside from licensing opportunities, supplying Hong Kong via our Malaysian licensee was the most viable option.

When I was based in Kuala Lumpur and later Seoul, I travelled frequently between the two licensees. As neither Korean nor Malaysian airlines flew direct between the cities, I used Cathay Pacific, which always involved an overnight stay in Hong Kong in each direction. For two years, I spent two nights a month there. Booking through Cathay secured excellent stopover rates.

I stayed in over thirty five-star hotels in Hong Kong, including the Hyatt Regency, Peninsula, Marco Polo, Hong Kong Hotel, New World, Ritz-Carlton and Hilton. The Hyatt Regency was my favourite location; the Peninsula was the most sumptuous.

The Hyatt had tailors and specialist shops on the ground floor. One was Shoeman Lau, who made me a pair of slip-on brogues with tassels instead of laces. They were magnificent. When I returned home, I wore them proudly to visit my sister.

The Export Adventurer

Her Alsatian cross greeted me enthusiastically and settled with his head resting on my feet.

When I stood up to leave half an hour later, a severed tassel dropped onto the carpet.

In those days, hotel service was extraordinary. Room boys on each floor would ask when you were returning so tea or coffee could be waiting. Nothing was too much trouble.

Hong Kong became even more important when I was based in Seoul. Korea had every meat and vegetable imaginable but lacked essential British staples such as Bisto gravy granules and HP Sauce—without which a bacon sandwich is a tragedy.

Marks & Spencer Food in Hong Kong was almost opposite the Hyatt. In many ways, it was more British than Britain. Jimmy's Kitchen served traditional British dishes so traditional I had only seen them in *The Dandy* and *The Beano*—round steak and kidney puddings, for instance.

Hong Kong had everything, for every taste.

The Export Adventurer

Chapter 28 — Taiwan

Formerly known as Formosa, Taiwan lies in the East China Sea, about halfway between Hong Kong and Korea. It was a regular stopping point for Cathay Pacific on the Hong Kong–Seoul route. Because I passed through so frequently, it became a natural market to explore.

On my first trip to Taipei, I was booked into the President Hotel, which was in an excellent location close to shops, restaurants, and bars. I used the President on every visit and stayed there on all twelve trips I made to Taiwan for Bartol-Hepworth.

Bill McGlinchey, the original CEO of Western Plastics in Texas, had provided our managing director with information on a company already extruding and injection-moulding polybutylene in Taiwan. This information dated back to the negotiations over the supply of PB to the UK at a meeting held at the Churchill Hotel in London in 1981. Before being acquired by Shell Chemicals, Western Plastics in Texas had been the original manufacturer and supplier of polybutylene resins.

The Taiwanese manufacturer, Taiwan Western, was owned by Dr Chiang. He and his team had developed a system of PB pipes with PB fittings and a thermostatically controlled device that reheated the inside of the fitting sockets and the outside of the pipe to melting point. When pushed

The Export Adventurer

together, the joint became permanently welded.

I could see significant problems with this system. It required an electrical supply during installation, and in damp or dirty site conditions there was a real risk of contamination of the weld. Initially, I had hoped that we might be able to sell Dr Chiang the technology for our push-fit fittings. However, after several visits, it became clear that he was perfectly satisfied with their own system.

Despite this, Dr Chiang and I became good friends. He and his team took great pleasure in entertaining me and showing me, with obvious pride, the highly industrialised island of Taiwan. We often went out for long lunches or dinners, which were invariably washed down with copious quantities of rice wine. As a result, afternoons were usually very sleepy affairs.

Some of the food available in Taipei was extraordinarily exotic. One street in particular, Snake Alley—also known as Huaxi Street Night Market—was located near the Mengjia Longshan Temple. It was lined with stands serving local snacks and restaurants offering traditional Taiwanese dishes, along with many delicacies not commonly found elsewhere.

These included snake blood and meat, turtle blood and meat, and deer penis wine. Many of the stalls specialised exclusively in snake-related delicacies and drinks—hence the nickname "Snake Alley".

Here, people displayed and slaughtered terrapins

and snakes in the most brutal fashion. Snake blood and a green liquid extracted from a gland within the snake were mixed with clear spirits or wine and offered to crowds of onlookers to sample. The snakes were split longitudinally using a pair of nail scissors to extract the blood and gland. It was not a pretty sight.

On another occasion, I was taken to a restaurant filled with aquaria containing large live frogs. You were expected to choose the frog you wanted to eat. Another restaurant served nothing but tripe—dozens of different varieties from many different animals. I have always prided myself on trying anything once, but I would never choose to return to either a frog restaurant or a tripe restaurant. On the whole, however, the food in Taiwan was excellent.

When Chiang Kai-shek withdrew in the face of Mao Tse-tung's Communist forces in mainland China, he and his army took millions of historical artefacts with them to Taiwan. Dr Chiang took great delight in guiding me around the vast, multi-storey modern building housing the National Palace Museum.

According to the literature, the artefacts on display were changed every few months and replaced with others from the immense stores and archives. They had so many artefacts that it would take over thirty years before each one would see the light of day again.

Among the most astonishing exhibits were entire cityscapes carved onto the surface of a tiny acorn. Viewed through a microscope, they revealed every detail of the streets and the population. It was almost unbelievable—there was so much detail that I had to look several times to convince myself it was real.

The Export Adventurer

After I left Bartol-Hepworth, Dr Chiang and I remained friends. During my later trading days with Korea Connections, he often helped me source Taiwan-produced products that I was looking for.

Chapter 29 — Thailand

Several local Thai companies were keen to obtain licences to manufacture the Acorn PB plumbing system. One evening, after a long day of meetings, I was taken on a tour of the city. We drove past the Royal Palace with its many golden domes and spires, enjoyed a delicious seafood and saffron rice meal, and, as the evening wore on, my host, Mr Orankjanan, insisted that I should experience what he described as a proper Thai massage.

We walked along a street lined with expansive shop windows. In one of them were rows of plinths of varying heights, the lowest running the entire width of the window at the front.

On each step sat three or four girls dressed in what could best be described as beautiful, colourful wedding dresses—pastel yellows, blues, oranges and purples, through to deep blues, reds, scarlets and jet black.

The Export Adventurer

Every girl was a beauty, ranging from under five feet to about five foot six, from petite to curvy. Each wore a numbered badge and, as I stood looking through the window, each in turn tried to catch my eye, smiling and striking a pose. Out of the eighteen or twenty on display, at least half a dozen drew my attention.

My host and I went inside, where he spoke briefly to the lady receptionist, who appeared to be in her mid-thirties (I have always had difficulty judging the ages of Asian women). Mr Orankjanan asked me whether I had chosen the number of the one I liked most. After a moment's hesitation, I settled on number 21.

We were shown into a lounge-bar area that would not have looked out of place in a four-star hotel. Mr Orankjanan ordered beers for both of us. He explained that the young lady I had chosen would shortly take me into another room for the massage, which could take two or three hours or more. If I finished before him, I was to return to the lounge and have another drink.

The beer arrived—a large jug and two glasses—and the waiter filled them and withdrew. Shortly afterwards, the young lady appeared. Mr Orankjanan spoke briefly with her and then introduced us.

"This is Miss Soo Mi, and this is Mr Bratley."

I stood and held out my hand. She smiled and shook it automatically.

She led me to the room, which could easily have belonged to a four-star hotel almost anywhere in the world. It was about six yards square, nicely carpeted, with a television, a dressing table and mirror, a small coffee table with two chairs, air conditioning, and a ceiling fan slowly stirring the air. The walls were papered and decorated with ornaments and pictures.

The more notable differences were a large round ceiling mirror positioned over a king-size circular bed, and a bathroom with no walls—a shower, WC, roll-top bath, and tiled floor with a drain. An inflated black lilo was propped casually against one wall.

Soo Mi smiled and…

…the massage began.

Some time later there was a knock at the door, and a smartly dressed waiter entered, balancing a tray with two bottles of beer and two glasses. He bowed, set them down calmly, collected the empties, and left. It was clearly all very routine.

The treatment continued, unhurried and expertly delivered, and by the time it ended I felt completely restored.

My host insisted on paying, although I had already tipped Soo Mi.

It was possibly the best massage I have ever had. I can quite understand why so many European men gravitate towards Thailand for their holidays.

In the end, we never tied up a deal in Thailand—not because of any lack of opportunity, but simply because I was already fully committed in Malaysia, Korea and New Zealand, and did not have the time required to nurture the interest properly.

Chapter 30 — South Korea

Whenever I went abroad on a visit, to mitigate costs I always tried to include as many nearby markets as possible. Chambers of Commerce, on the other hand, with their trade mission programmes, usually visited only one market. Most delegates flew as a group, direct to and from the target country.

Because of my earlier experience at BNA–Gowanbury, I was already conditioned to carry out market visits as cost-effectively as possible. It made little sense to me to spend seventeen hours flying to Hong Kong, remain in the transit lounge for a few hours, and then fly on to Seoul, Tokyo, Beijing, or Taipei. Hong Kong—still a British colony at the time—was always worth a look, and most Cathay Pacific flights from Hong Kong to Seoul or Tokyo stopped en route in Taipei, Taiwan.

On my first trade mission to Seoul, I travelled three or four days ahead of the main delegation and spent those days in Hong Kong. I had done my research and met with the sales agents involved in the Johnson GRP mains water-supply pipes that brought Hong Kong's water from China.

Paul Au was keen to add the Bartol and Hepworth industrial product ranges to his portfolio. We immediately began receiving orders, particularly from British military installations. There were numerous British Army, Navy, Air Force and Marine barracks, dockyards, airfields, hospitals, schools and administrative buildings.

In Taipei, I met Dr Chiang of Taiwan Western for the first time—a relationship that would continue for many years.

The Export Adventurer

My first arrival in Seoul was about two hours behind the main mission group. We were staying at the super-deluxe, city-centre Hotel Lotte. During check-in, I was handed a large A4 envelope containing mission information from the Chamber of Commerce. After being escorted to my room, I tipped the bellboy ₩2,000 and spent the next few minutes wondering how much money I had actually given him.

I turned on the television and flicked through the channels until I found AFKN—the American Forces Korea Network. To my surprise, the recently released film *Chariots of Fire* was just starting.

The phone rang. A thickly accented female voice said,

"Herro Mr Blateley, you alive arone, you rike rady company?"

Assuming it was a fellow mission joker, I replied, "Yes, send two."

Five minutes later, there was a knock at the door. Expecting to see one or more mission members, I opened it—only to find two beautifully dressed young women standing there.

That was my first introduction to South Korea.

I never imagined it would be the first of so many visits, or the beginning of a love affair with the country that would last the rest of my working life.

Among the documents in the A4 envelope was the itinerary for the Embassy briefing, a formal reception, and the final debriefing on the last day.

We gathered in the lobby and were met by a member of the Embassy's commercial staff, who guided us on the ten-minute walk from the Lotte to the British Embassy via the underpasses near City Hall railway station. After the usual briefing with Ambassador David Hughes, I set off around Seoul visiting contractors on my list. In hindsight, it generated little immediate interest, but it was not time wasted.

One of the engineers I met introduced me to Mr Kang Hok Seng, the principal architect with Korea Condominiums, who owned holiday hotels and condominium developments across Korea. Mr Kang already had our Acorn polybutylene plumbing system brochure on file.

He was interested in the system because he believed it would be less prone to rupture caused by vibration from seismic activity. Korea Condominiums were considering developments near Japan, on the boundary of two major tectonic plates, where earth movements were common.

We began in South Korea with a very modest initial order for Acorn polybutylene pipes and fittings—hardly enough to justify the cost of the trip, but it was a step in the right direction.

Over the following months, Mr Kang began making modest sales beyond Korea Condominiums, and contractors were impressed by the simplicity of installation.

We appointed Korea Condominiums as our sole agent for Acorn in Korea. They worked hard, but there was one major drawback: existing plumbing systems—galvanised iron,

The Export Adventurer

copper, stainless steel and various plastic solvent-weld and compression systems—were all imperial-sized and made to Korean equivalents of American ASTM standards.

I joined another trade mission to Seoul, linked to an exhibition sponsored by the BOTB at the Korean World Trade Centre in Gangnam. We exhibited our products, and interest in the Acorn polybutylene push-fit system increased markedly.

Korean business culture expects staff to socialise together. It is normal for a company president or vice president to take all office staff out on Friday or Saturday evenings. Much of this entertainment takes place in room salons.

Each evening, Mr Kang and his Vice President, Mr Lee Young Nam, took me to dinner and then on to either a Norebang (karaoke room) or a room salon.

Norebang was harmless fun—except that everyone was expected to sing, and I do not possess a good singing voice.

Room salons were another matter entirely.

A typical room salon consisted of a small private room, perhaps eight metres by four. Half the room contained a U-shaped banquette surrounding a low table; the other half was covered in traditional varnished paper flooring.

Each man was paired with a young woman who sat close, poured drinks, peeled fruit and danced if asked. Both men and women drank. The staple drink at the time was a Scotch whisky specially blended for Korea—Blackstone.

The girls filled the shot glasses. After drinking, the custom was to pass the empty glass to someone else, refill theirs, and repeat the cycle. A classic party trick involved everyone passing their glasses to the guest simultaneously—leaving him with eight full shots to drink before anyone else could continue.

As the evening progressed and a second or third bottle was consumed, the door would open and a man would enter pushing a karaoke machine. Drinking stopped, singing commenced, and eight increasingly intoxicated people would perform enthusiastically until two or three in the morning, when the room salon closed.

Some went home. Many took their companions to nearby hotels that charged by the hour.

I found this cultural duality confusing. Every Korean I met was deeply family-oriented, devoted to wife and children, and often strongly religious—yet office nights out followed a very different code. What happened in the room salon stayed there.

Another common diversion was the barbershop.

When I first arrived in Korea, I was amazed at how many barbers there were—seemingly one on every block. My first visit was with Mr Lee, who took me into a new office block in Youido. We descended into the basement where a barbershop operated.

Shoes were removed, slippers donned, and we were led into a private room with two American-style barber chairs. Ties were removed, shirt collars folded inward, and two barbers began work.

After the haircut, the chairs reclined, legs were elevated, feet were washed, dried meticulously, and toenails trimmed. Hot towels softened my face before a careful straight-razor shave, followed by cucumber slices and a facial pack.

I was then laid flat and given a thorough massage of hands, arms, legs, back, shoulders and abdomen.

At one point, I felt my belt being unbuckled…

She made it plain that further services were available, should I wish.

I later learned that a barbershop with a single pole offered only grooming services; multiple poles indicated a wider menu.

Hoping I did not grow weary of haircuts, late nights and early mornings, we continued our aggressive marketing push.

It became clear that sales would accelerate dramatically if we could offer American-standard products. Manufacturing those sizes in the UK was prohibitively expensive, so local production became inevitable.

Mr Kang was a member of Yonggi Cho's Youido Full Gospel Church, the largest Pentecostal church in the world. He had many friends and associates who would help him. The church on the island of Youido in the Han River had, in the early 1980s, an entire congregation of half a million members. The church could accommodate 30,000 people at a time, with numerous back-to-back services all day on Sundays.

The Export Adventurer

Mr Kang showed Acorn around, and many of the church's business members were interested and prepared to back him.

With sufficient funding to commence local manufacture under licence, Mr Kang resigned from Korea Condominiums and set up Korea Bartol.

We not only needed a licence document acceptable to the Bartol Plastics board of directors on one side and Mr Kang and his backers on the other, but also an agreement that the Korean Ministry of Trade, Industry and Energy would approve.

Bartol-Hepworth's solicitors in the UK wanted to start from a draft licence on their word processor, which would have required extensive negotiation to pass the Ministry. I instead took the Ministry's draft licence and, after a few negotiated additions and deletions, produced a fair, clear agreement acceptable to all parties.

The draft was sent back to the UK, who asked for minor clarifications, which were added. Their lawyers then returned a completely new draft—so full of holes and ambiguities that it would have been a litigation nightmare if anything went wrong.

Fortunately, Mike Marsden was still in charge at Bartol Plastics. He took a pragmatic approach and approved the Ministry-based licence, which protected both our technology and income.

The licence allowed Koreans to manufacture and sell within Korea, while allowing Bartol UK to purchase Korean-made products for markets using American standards, such as Taiwan, the Philippines and the USA. Bartol UK immediately began buying tube secateurs and other ancillaries from Korea.

The Export Adventurer

I was still based in the UK and took part in another trade mission organised by the Huddersfield Chamber of Commerce, with whom I had been to India a couple of years earlier. Roger Nunns was now leading most of Huddersfield Chamber's missions, so it was terrific to meet up with him again. We were in Korea over the weekend. Mr Kang arranged for us to stay at the Korea Condominium on Cheju Island. We flew off for a fabulous weekend touring the volcanic island.

On that same mission, I took Roger around The Secret Garden at Changdeokgung Palace in Seoul. After looking around what used to be the Kings of Korea's residences and gardens, we completed our tour by 2 PM. we were both hungry.

I suggested a nearby Bulgogi (BBQ beef) restaurant. Roger's response was very negative. He disliked Korean food and particularly hated Korean pickles (kimchi). He suggested a restaurant underneath the Lotte Hotel, the 'Bobby London', which specialised in roast beef and Yorkshire puddings. I told Roger, "I know a place where you can get roast beef, Yorkshire pudding, mashed potatoes, glazed carrots,

The Export Adventurer

Brussels sprouts followed by jam roly-poly and custard" Roger's eyes lit up, and he asked where. I answered, "at the Redbeck in Wakefield, Roger, but we are in Seoul right now". It did not work! Thirty minutes later, we were in the Bobby London.

On another occasion, when George Bell was with me, Mr Kang again arranged for us to visit the Korea condominium on Cheju Island. George and I hired a car with a driver and travelled around Cheju do (island).

The island is covered in lots of extinct conical volcanoes, and at one place, it is possible to walk half a mile through an underground natural lava tube, where the outer crust had set, but the molten lava inside had drained away, leaving the huge, cavernous system.

We reached the southern corner of the island at lunchtime and, with the driver's help, found a fish restaurant.

Had we been on our own in a hired car, we would not have known that it was a restaurant, there were no signs outside, and the appearance was identical to the other farmsteads dotted around.

The Export Adventurer

The only difference was a large 2m x 2m x 0.6m deep, best described as a giant 'Belfast sink' outside the entrance door, which we discovered contained live sea bass.

We were met by the host, who spoke no English. Still, with gesticulations and other body language, we soon understood that he wanted us to choose a fish, which we did.

Inside the restaurant, the decor and style were entirely traditional. We removed our shoes and tried to don the slippers far too small for us. We were taken into one of several rooms with varnished paper flooring. The only furniture was a 9-inch-high table and cushions. I have consumed several meals over the years, sitting cross-legged in front of a very low table. However, because of my rugby and skiing-damaged knees, I have always found it an uncomfortable trial after more than thirty minutes.

After settling down the best way we could on the cushions, we decided that as we were in such traditional surroundings and were not driving, we would order the potent local rice wine.

The table soon filled with a multitude of dishes with various forms of Korean kimchi, Chinese cabbage, Cubed Radish Kimchi, Ponytail Radish, Cucumber, Red Water, Radish Water, Kimchi, and Mustard Leaf Kimchi, to name a few. There were plates of various salad leaves and a bowl of pickled garlic cloves.

There were many condiments, including soy sauce and wasabi mustard, which both George and I knew needed mixing in the dish provided to produce the dipping sauce.

After only a few minutes, the fish was brought in. It was laid on a large oval plate on a bed of shredded cabbage. The head and the tail had been left on the fish's skeleton. All the flesh from the sides had been removed, cut into small chopstick manageable strips, and arranged neatly on top.

As George reached out with his chopsticks to take the first piece of fish, the fish's mouth opened, and it lifted its tail from the bed of cabbage. We both looked on in astonishment that it was still alive. George paused and said, "I feel like a cannibal," but took a piece of the flesh and dunked it in the soy/wasabi sauce.

The Export Adventurer

It was indeed fresh and delicious, but I would have preferred it to have been dead before they brought it onto the table.

I loved trying new foods; a hundred raw ready, shelled oysters were just a few dollars in any Korean supermarket. Prawns, octopus, squid, and fish, either cooked or raw, served as sashimi, were plentiful and easily found in restaurants.

On one occasion, I tried Sannakji (Raw octopus). It is a Korean delicacy. It is like sushi, except they take a live octopus or squid and slice it up immediately before serving it to the table. Although it is dead, the tentacles are still squirming, making it appear alive. You can feel the suction cups grasping at your teeth and tongue as soon as you put them in your mouth.

Another exotic dish, Dalkbal, is a whole chicken foot, bones all coated in a chilli batter and deep fried. Once it is in your mouth, you scrape off the little bit of meat on the bone with your teeth. Dalkbal is one of the spiciest dishes in Korea. The combination of a chicken foot in your mouth and mind-numbing spiciness requires a certain level of bravery for even the most experienced Korean food connoisseurs.

They also have other strange-looking foods like the larvae of the silkworm, often sold from large bowls in the street or the dried grasshoppers offered as nibbles in many bars. I have tried them, and they do taste a little nutty, but please give me real nuts every time.

Many people comment on the fact that Koreans are famous for eating dogs. The dog they eat is a special breed bred for that sole purpose, and the ownership of all the other breeds as loved pets is just as prevalent in Korea as in the UK. As an animal lover, I still have difficulty understanding the Korean psyche on this matter.

During those early days of developing the Korean market, I took part in several trade missions, on one occasion staying in the Lotte, the Hyatt Regency, then the Hilton hotel, and the Westin Chosun, all of which had their nightclubs, the Rainforest in the Hilton, and the Xanadu under the Chosun.

Itaewon, with its many bars and its American GI clientele, was a short taxi ride away, where Stevie Wonder was belting out "I just called to say I love you" with, without exaggeration, hundreds of the most beautiful young women vying for your attention. It was a man's paradise, especially for a lonely man in a disintegrating marriage.

Once the business gravitated around to licensed manufacturing, I stayed in the Garden Hotel in Mapo dong (later it became the Holiday Inn) because it was the nearest high-class hotel to Mr Kangs' office in Youido. It was also often used by the American Army for visiting senior military personnel.

I was awaiting a taxi at the front of the hotel with a representative from Catnic in Wales. We were both exhibiting at the World Trade Centre in Kang Nam, and both of us had hired interpreters. As we were waiting for the taxi, we were discussing our interpreters and their command of the English language when a senior American officer (*with so many medals and decorations on his chest, I thought they must invent them, Perhaps one for getting up early, another for shaving in cold water, etc.*) Interjected into our conversation, "don't you mean their American is very good" and the Welsh guy, sharp as a button, responded, "I have no idea; no one we have met so far was speaking in Apache, Cheyenne, Sioux or any other American language."

When I was not with the other mission members, drinking in the hotel or the Itaewon bars, Mr Kang and Mr Lee often took me to dinner, followed by visits to room salons, massage parlours and barbershops.

One evening in the Rainforest disco in the Hilton, I met a very pretty young lady Miss Yun Se Hee. She was small even by Korean standards, standing at about five'2", and I saw her on and off every time I visited Korea for the best part of the next 18 months.

When the license was signed and the plant and tooling were in production, the Koreans started a marketing drive to bring the product to the attention of the specifiers and users of construction products in Korea.

They took me all over Korea, meeting the leading architects, consultants, engineers, and contractors. They kept me out until the early hours of every morning. I was getting more tired each day, and they were getting to understand more of the technical things about the product and its installation. They referred to me less and less in the 'all Korean language meetings.' It was quite a challenge sometimes not to fall asleep.

One lunchtime, they announced that we were going to Pusan the next day, so we were not going out that evening. I breathed a sigh of relief because I could get some much-needed sleep.

The Export Adventurer

I also was pleased because if we were flying, it would have taken an hour. I could sleep, if we went by train, it was four hours, more sleep and if it were by car, five hours, even more sleep so I enquired how we were travelling, and they responded: "by train". They dropped me off at 5 PM at my hotel; I ordered a club sandwich and coffee from room service and was awaiting delivery when the phone rang. It was Miss Cho from the office who spoke excellent English. Mr Kang and Mr Lee had forgotten to tell me that we were leaving earlier than usual for the railway station. Instead of being ready at 8 AM, I needed to be ready to leave at 7:30 AM. However, Miss Cho (like all Koreans) did not want to put me out if she could help it. So, the conversation started like, "hello, Mr Gerry, what time is your morning erection?" I almost fell off the chair with amusement. Still, I managed to resist the most obvious response. I confirmed I would be ready and waiting for them.

Policing any licensed manufacturing unit is important to ensure the correct royalties are collected. In Korea, this was made very simple because there was only one worldwide manufacturer of polybutylene resin at the time, and that was Shell Chemicals in Houston, Texas, with whom I had already negotiated an agreement for Shell to share with us information on any sales to our licensees.

Setting up the factory in Korea was no mean feat; we had to set up a production line for the PB (polybutylene) pipe, which involved a piece of technology central to the technology transfer on how to manufacture the tube to the tolerances required.

Both the pipe's O/D (outside diameter) and the bore (inside diameter) had to be manufactured within extremely tight tolerances. The O/D had to fit tightly and snugly into the O-ring to make the watertight seal and the stainless-steel grab ring to stop it from blowing out under pressure. The bore had to snugly and tightly accept a stainless tube end steel liner.

In those days, if you looked down the bore of most extruded plastic pipes, you would observe slight undulations. The undulations were caused by tiny variations in the die head pressure where the molten plastic was being forced through the die head. Either by applying positive pressure inside the pipe or negative pressure (vacuum) on the outside of the pipe as it passed through a series of calibration plates, the O/D of the pipe always remained smooth and consistent within the manufacturing tolerances as it cooled and hardened, but the bore and wall thickness were both slightly variable.

The technology was on how to iron out those variations in die head pressure so that both the O/D and bore of the pipe could be both dimensionally consistent. The answer was to add a unique piece of kit; a Swiss-made Maag die head pump.

We also had to supply the Koreans with a complete set of injection moulding tool drawings to manufacture the fittings, but PB (polybutylene) had another unusual property in that unlike most other thermoplastics, which, when cooled are entirely finished, PB, when cooled had the consistency of hard chewing gum and did not fully cure for two or three days. This slow curing meant that you did not fully know what you had manufactured for some time.

Because of the sticky properties of the injection moulded finished product, the moulding tools had to be Teflon (non-stick) coated. Otherwise, the moulding could be damaged by the ejection mechanism.

Polybutylene was new material to the Korean Injection Mould Tool manufacturing company, and they were unaware of how different it was from other thermoplastics. They thought they could save Korea-Bartol some money by leaving out the Teflon coating. This omission proved a disastrous waste of money. It caused a three-month delay in production until new Teflon-coated moulds could be manufactured.

At the same time, the extrusion line was ready to run, and I requested the assistance of an engineer from Bartol-Hepworth in Doncaster to commission the line. He turned up, and converted ten tonnes of brand-new PB resin, bought from Shell in Houston, into scrap before getting any usable product.

This incident was not the only Technology transfer blunder. During one of my infrequent trips back to the UK, I asked for the drawings and specifications for the stainless-steel components. Neither Bartol-Hepworth's' research and development nor production departments could furnish the information.

What was quite frightening was that the R&D technical manager had already been dubbed the nickname Mr Teflon because no blame or responsibility ever stuck to him. The grab rings and liners had been developed on behalf of Bartol-Hepworth by a specialised division of British Steel. Only British Steel had the necessary drawings and information to replicate the product in Korea.

The Export Adventurer

The material was 18/8 stainless steel, and by careful measurement of a diverse selection of samples, we were able to establish the dimensional tolerances and then apply those to the Korea/USA sizes we were making.

It became quite clear very quickly, that Bartol-Hepworth must have developed the PB pipe and fittings production following a concept, and eventually created the finished product after a long series of trial and error.

I took careful notes of everything, including the die head and injection mould tool drawings. I built a complete "transfer of technology" manual. So, should we have to repeat licensing in the future, all the information was in one place?

George and I decided that as I was travelling backwards and forwards between Malaysia and Korea every month, perhaps it would be better if I were to be based in Korea, where I could keep an eye on developments on a day-to-day basis.

We did not wish to discourage the Koreans from looking for possible savings. Korea was already very industrially developed, and it was probable that some savings could be made. However, when suggestions arose, I could obtain input from the technical and production teams back in Doncaster.

I also had to agree to the proposed changes and a future support package with Bina Bartol in Kuala Lumpur before the move became permanent.

Mr Kang was delighted when I informed him that I would move my East Asia base from Kuala Lumpur to Seoul. He felt he had to entertain me, so at least twice a week, we were out in room salons and bars enjoying what Seoul had to offer.

The Koreans also thought it would be helpful to me to have a bilingual secretary, and they advertised for and received about twenty applicants for the post. Mr Kang left it to me to interview each and choose the one with whom I would be most comfortable. I decided on Mrs Cho Hye Young, who had returned home to her mother's home in Korea a few months prior, to have her and her Los Angeles-based husbands' baby. It is customary in Korea for young mothers to do this. However, in the 2 to 3 months she was away, he had started a relationship with another Korean in LA.

Her English was excellent, and I probably gave her the job because I empathised with her situation. However, what I did not realise at the time was that both being in similar situations, we often discussed our problems, and this led us into a personal relationship. Mrs Cho was a Christian, and it is normal in Korea for Christians to adopt a Christian name; she had chosen Dominique.

The Export Adventurer

I was in the process of house hunting in Seoul and put Miss Cho on the case, she found an excellent new four-bedroomed apartment in the east of the city, very close to Songsu Bridge, and we moved in.

The transfer of technology was successful. Within six months of signing the licence, we were making PB pipe and fittings in Korea to the American copper tube standard ASTM B88 outside diameters in ½ inch, ¾ inch and 1-inch nominal sizes. Manufacturing three dimensions were quite an achievement because the UK factory was still only making the 15 and 22-mm sizes.

The process had been so much cheaper in Korea, and the demand for the larger sizes was so much lower than for 15 and 22 mm, that it was muted that it may be cheaper to produce the 28 mm pipe and fittings in Korea for the UK.

Unfortunately, back in the UK, Hepworth Ceramic Holdings were on another of their endless cost-cutting exercises, any duplicated functions were merged, and skills and experience were consigned to redundancy. Savings temporally showed up on the balance sheet as extra profit, driving up the share value.

However, the long-term effect of losing the expertise was a nosedive in the quality of service, which inevitably led to reduced overall sales. Short-termism and stock exchange ranking have been the death knell of British industry over the last half-century.

In 1986 the third MD/CEO of Bartol Plastics Ltd was retired early and replaced by Hepworth Ceramic Holdings, imposing a fourth chief executive in three years. For me, it was the final straw. The mother business in the UK was no longer stable, and living out in East Asia meant that none of the new executives knew who I was. I had lost confidence in the encumbered now looking after export when I was based in Malaysia.

Communication was still a problem. The CEO/MD at Bartol Plastics Ltd had a fax machine in his office. The alternative was telex, which could be read by all and sundry before it got to the addressee. I arranged with another returning British businessman to carry back a letter, which he posted in London a day or so later. The letter was my notice of resignation, effective in one month.

The Telex and the fax machine were white hot for the next couple of days, requesting that I return to the UK for talks, which I agreed to do, providing Bartol-Hepworth paid for the return Seoul-London-Seoul return ticket. The talks initially focussed on trying to get me to withdraw my resignation, but they soon realised that was never going to happen, so the negotiations turned to protecting their technology. I had no intention of misusing their intellectual property and was very happy to agree to accept a sum of around £5000 in exchange for signing an agreement not to use my knowledge of their products to anyone else's benefit.

I returned to Korea two weeks later, and Dominique moved us into an apartment in Inchon.

Chapter 31 — Alexy/Aronstead

By 1987, I realised I had created a monster. The Korean, Malaysian and New Zealand licensees constantly called on my time, and other agents and distributors throughout East Asia kept in close touch.

Without help, I thought I would eventually burn myself out—until an opportunity emerged from an unexpected direction.

The trade missions to India and South Korea with the Huddersfield Chamber of Commerce had been led by their export manager, Roger Nunns. It was through Roger that a chance arose to represent Alexy/Aronstead.

Roger's brother, Mike, was the sales manager for Alexy Toys, and at that time they held the contract to supply the BBC Children in Need Pudsey Bear. The quantities were beginning to outstrip their own manufacturing capacity, and they wanted to find a high-quality production source. South Korea was then the world's leading producer of high-quality plush soft toys.

I made a few phone calls around Seoul and soon had sales representatives beating a path to my office. I supplied each of them with samples, drawings and specifications, and the quotations and samples rained in. Buying, it turned out, could be a lot easier than selling.

Next, Alexy's sister company, Aronstead, asked me to source suitcases, keep-fit equipment and leather handbags for their Argos supply contracts. I put together a range of suitcases, obtained dozens of handbag samples, and shipped them off to Aronstead. Within weeks, I received orders for a container-load of rowing and jogging machines, and two containers of mixed handbags.

The Export Adventurer

One amusing recollection was my concern about mechanical breakdowns on the keep-fit equipment. During a meeting with the Taiwanese manufacturer, I raised durability and spare parts. He replied that most keep-fit equipment is bought, used a few times, then put away and never touched again. Warranty claims, he said, were almost non-existent—and on the rare occasion something did fail, they simply replaced the whole unit.

Alexy/Aronstead offered me a package to act as their buying agent in East Asia, which I decided to accept. I signed the contract in early October, to start on 1 December 1987.

I moved into a new modern apartment in Chungdong, halfway between Seoul and Inchon, and remained in Korea until the end of the Seoul Olympic Games in 1988.

My parents were both in their late seventies. My father had been diagnosed with bowel cancer and successfully treated, but I did not want to be so far away should anything happen to either of them. So, in August 1988, I returned to the UK.

I looked around and, although many export sales roles were offered, I avoided anything that involved extensive overseas travel.

Chapter 32 — Allied Dunbar

I chanced upon a sales associate from Allied Dunbar who had sold me an endowment policy some years earlier. During our conversation, it struck me that working from home as a financial adviser might suit me very well.

I passed the interviews and induction exams without difficulty and was sent to Swindon for two consecutive weeks of basic training.

The training was comprehensive. At Allied Dunbar's head office in Swindon, the emphasis was firmly on squeaky-clean ethics and the principle of giving "best advice" from the customer's perspective. However, once back at the local branch, the emphasis shifted dramatically towards sales.

League tables were updated daily, showing each sales associate's performance both monthly and annually. Those languishing at the bottom endured considerable embarrassment, while those at the top enjoyed inflated egos.

Seniority was based exclusively on commission earned. Those at the bottom of the league were simply "sales associates" and could use any spare desk when they visited the office. The next grade up, earning more than £25,000 per annum in commission, were designated *Kestrels* and were allocated permanent desk space.

Above them were the *Falcons*, earning over £50,000 per annum, who occupied larger and quieter areas of the open-plan office. At the top were *Senior Falcons*, earning over £75,000 per annum, each with their own private office.

Every sales associate was responsible for generating their own leads. This meant selling insurance, investment and pension products first to friends, relatives and neighbours before moving on to the general public. Many failed at this stage, having exhausted their personal networks and discovered their unsuitability for the role.

The training emphasised extracting referrals from each client, but friends of friends and relatives of friends were soon depleted. At that point, telemarketing became unavoidable.

The insurance company loaned new sales associates money to keep them afloat until their commission accruals overtook their drawings. Only then, in theory, could they begin repaying the loans. In practice, anyone who discovered they were not suited to the role found they could not leave until the debt was repaid.

Allied Dunbar showed no mercy in pursuing outstanding debts. Several former associates were driven into bankruptcy.

Telemarketing involved either working through the telephone directory—resulting in appointments scattered across a wide geographical area—or calling street by street from the electoral roll. I found telemarketing particularly challenging.

Forty years ago, people were generally more polite than they are today. At the time, telemarketing usually meant double glazing or fitted kitchens, so although unsolicited calls were unwelcome, outright abuse was rare. Most people believed they were already financially well covered. Our approach was to offer a free financial-planning "check-up".

The success rate was roughly one appointment for every twelve calls. To secure twenty appointments a week, one needed to make at least 240 prospecting calls.

The Export Adventurer

Once inside a client's home, the first step was a detailed fact-find of their finances. The second was to explain any vulnerabilities:

1. If they died, was their family adequately protected?
2. Would their pensions provide sufficient income in retirement if they lived?
3. How would they cope if illness or injury prevented them from working?

The final step: roughly one in four clients would sign up for at least one financial product.

Looking back, I now describe the sales process as:

1. *Hitch 'em* — securing the appointment
2. *Pitch 'em* — outlining worst-case scenarios
3. *Stitch 'em* — getting the signature

It was the most disgraceful and unethical business I have ever been involved in.

LAUTRO (the Life Assurance and Unit Trust Regulatory Organisation, a forerunner of the FSA) permitted insurance companies to project future pension and investment growth at rates of 8½% and 11%. In reality, most policies have struggled to achieve even 5%.

This created a grossly distorted picture for investors, savers and pension holders.

Many people were encouraged to transfer out of final-salary pension schemes into private pensions offered by Allied Dunbar and others, based on these LAUTRO-approved projections. Many ended up with pensions far smaller than those they would have received had they left their arrangements untouched.

The blame did not lie with individual sales associates; it lay with the insurance companies and LAUTRO itself. I know several associates who transferred their own pensions to Allied Dunbar—to their eventual detriment.

Many people today still have interest-only mortgages supported by endowment policies that were supposedly designed to repay the loan. They now find those endowments are worth only a fraction of what was promised at the point of sale.

Ironically, I did very well at Allied Dunbar. I achieved Kestrel status in my first year and enjoyed being entertained by Barbara Dickson at the Hyatt Hotel, Hyde Park Corner. In my second year, I achieved Falcon status.

That year, we were entertained by Rowan Atkinson at the Grosvenor House Hotel and then whisked off—with my wife—to Vancouver. There, we enjoyed an all-expenses-paid week touring British Columbia by coach and steam train, with Tom Jones providing the evening entertainment.

It was a wonderful holiday. One day we flew by seaplane to a lake in the Rockies for lunch; another day we visited Vancouver Island; another took us by steam train to Whistler. We watched log-felling and wood-carving competitions and went white-water rafting. One evening, Gastown was cordoned off exclusively for us, and vouchers were provided for food and drink in every bar and restaurant.

These conventions and incentives were carefully designed to feed the egos of the greedy. Make no mistake—so-called "Financial Services" often operate with the ethics of vultures,

The Export Adventurer

serving themselves rather than their clients. It was entirely appropriate that Allied Dunbar chose birds of prey as symbols of achievement.

Having earned £27,000 in my first year and £53,000 in my second, my accruals finally equalled my drawings by the third month of my third year. At that point, I chose to leave and seek a more ethical way of earning a living.

Chapter 33 — Barnsley Chamber of Commerce

In November 1991, Roger Nunns told me he had left the Huddersfield Chamber of Commerce and had become Chief Executive of Barnsley Chamber of Commerce and Industry.

He explained that the Chamber had previously been a part-time operation, opening only at set hours to issue certificates of origin and other documentation. However, new and more dynamic committee members had decided the town needed a full-time chamber.

Barnsley Town Council had made the old police station available on a peppercorn rent, and the Chamber Council had recruited Roger to run the new full-time organisation. By then, Roger had employed four or so permanent staff and was keen to establish an export department.

He asked whether I would join him if he could find the funding. It did not take long: within two weeks he had secured support from the Barnsley and Doncaster Training and Enterprise Council. Soon afterwards I received a written offer—a decent salary and a car—to create a Barnsley and Doncaster Export Association.

It was the start of an enjoyable interlude in my working life. I was home with my family every evening and was no longer chasing short-term goals.

The first thing I did was set up export clubs, starting in the newly opened Metrodome in Barnsley. We circulated all five hundred Chamber members and advertised the event in the local press. At the first club, over 150 people attended. Some were completely new to exporting, while others—particularly several mining equipment manufacturers—already had a history of international trade.

Over the next few months, attendance distilled down to around thirty regulars, all new or relatively new to exporting. I worked through them one at a time, establishing their needs and helping them get started.

The Doncaster Export Club followed soon afterwards, meeting monthly at the St Leger Hotel. As in Barnsley, the first event was packed, but over time the numbers reduced to a nucleus of regular members.

I had just about got on top of the workload generated by the export clubs when the Department of Trade and Industry office in Leeds suggested that the service was needed across the whole of South Yorkshire. They offered 50% funding if we extended the service to include the memberships of Rotherham and Sheffield Chambers of Commerce.

Rotherham welcomed the additional service and immediately established a monthly export breakfast club. Sheffield was more hesitant. They made positive noises, but they did not like the idea of an Export Development Service—and an Export Development Adviser—based in Barnsley having access to Sheffield businesses.

Sheffield Chamber of Commerce had always been one of the larger chambers. It was the only one in South Yorkshire that ran trade missions, issued ATA carnets, and had employed an Export Manager for many years. However, it had never been closely involved in the sales and marketing side of exporting, which was the main focus of the Export Development Service.

The Export Adventurer

This was also the period when Michael Heseltine, then Chair of the Board of Trade, announced that Chambers of Commerce should become more like the European model—large and powerful organisations. Many smaller chambers would need to merge to achieve this, and discussions were already under way: Barnsley with Doncaster, and Sheffield with Rotherham. Similar conversations were taking place across the UK.

Progress was, unsurprisingly, slow. Chief Executives negotiating mergers were effectively meeting to decide which of them might end up redundant. When the government changed in 1997, mergers were no longer a priority and the whole agenda was quietly postponed.

A typical working week for me was two days in the office dealing with administration and three days visiting Chamber members around South Yorkshire.

There was always a little rivalry between the four chambers. On one occasion, the Chief Executive of Rotherham Chamber told me they wanted export consultancy delivered "in a particular way that would suit Rotherham businesses".

I readily agreed—by then I had learned the politics—and asked Rotherham to define the differences between Rotherham businesses and the rest of South Yorkshire. Once I understood those differences, I told them, I would make the necessary adjustments.

As everyone involved in international trade knows, it is the end customer's requirements, destination-market rules and regulations, international contract terms, freight and insurance costs, and UK export licensing, tax and customs entry rules that dictate how you trade—not the exporter's location.

Another problem in those days was the sheer number of business-support organisations. Barnsley, for example, had an Economic Development Unit, a Business and Innovation Centre, a Training and Enterprise Council office, and the Chamber of Commerce. All provided "business advice", but each had different access criteria and varying levels of support.

Businesses had to take their needs to each organisation in turn to see who could help them most. Eventually, the government made the Training and Enterprise Councils the main fund holders for business support and merged services into a one-stop shop.

Alongside building a credible export consultancy across South Yorkshire, I was drawn into other work. Sheffield University decided to run a Business Administration course which included a module on international trade, and they asked me to deliver it.

They supplied the course notes which—ironically—covered European trade before we joined the EEC, so the content was outdated. When I pointed this out, they asked me to deliver it as written because the examination was based on the existing curriculum.

On another occasion, Barnsley's town twinning department asked whether I would accompany them to their twin town in eastern Ukraine. Horlivka is a steel and coal-mining city about ten miles from Donetsk. Ukraine had gained independence from the USSR only months before our visit.

The economy was still based on large state-owned organisations such as coal mines and steelworks, and there were virtually no manufacturing SMEs at all.

The Export Adventurer

I travelled to Horlivka with John Price from Barnsley's Economic Development Unit. Our brief was to help the economic development team within the Horlivka City Soviet (Council) establish support for small and medium-sized enterprises so that they could emerge and thrive.

We flew to Kyiv via Vienna, took a twelve-hour, trundling, Škoda-built sleeper train from Kyiv to Donetsk, then drove on to Horlivka. Donetsk and Horlivka were classic communist towns: tall, grey, drab housing blocks set back from wide boulevard roads. Moskvich's, Ladas and trams made up most of the traffic. Our City Council Volga limousine was something of a rarity.

On the way in and out, we managed an overnight stay in Kyiv each time—a magnificent city of golden-domed buildings perched above steep banks overlooking the river.

I visited Horlivka three times in six months. On the first trip there were fifteen roubles (coupons) to the pound; on the second, six hundred; on the third, six thousand.

It was a disaster for people on fixed incomes, such as retired miners. Many had enjoyed relatively high incomes before independence, but with the collapse of the currency what had once bought a week's groceries would, after only six months, buy a single potato.

Before independence, all the steel produced by the steelworks was loaded onto trains and shipped back into Russia every week. After independence, the trains ceased to arrive. The steelworks, however, continued production, stockpiling output until the fields around the plant were filled with steel.

The Export Adventurer

The sad thing was that senior management did not see sales or transport as their responsibility. They had been conditioned to believe they were responsible only for production.

We visited an aero-engine plant which, until the break-up of the USSR, had made turboprop engines for Russian aircraft manufacturers. It had now converted to making jewellery using the platinum and titanium stocks it held.

Every visit to every factory—including the steelworks, the coal mines and the aero-engine plant—ended the same way: a fresh bottle of vodka was opened in the General Manager's office and fully consumed before we were allowed to leave. On one or two occasions we were offered local beer that was 19° proof. No wonder the Russians were at the top of the worldwide alcoholism league tables.

As a small example of the impact of currency collapse, I decided to have a haircut and our escort, Eugene—who had been a KGB officer in Latvia before independence—took me to a hairdresser. Before we went in, he stressed that I was to pay only what was asked, because leaving a tip would, in a small way, add to spiralling inflation.

The hairdresser shampooed, cut and blow-dried my hair, gave me a neck and head massage, provided coffee and Turkish delight, and then reeled off the bill in roubles. I faithfully peeled off the notes. As I walked back down the street towards City Hall, I realised the entire experience had cost less than £0.02.

On another occasion, John and I went up to the bar on the top floor of the Stirol Hotel. We asked for two beers and were told they had run out. All they had was vodka and Crimean Champanski (champagne). We chose champagne as it was the least alcoholic option available and we were both already concerned about how much we had been drinking.

The Export Adventurer

When the champagne arrived at our table, it came with a glass bowl of Swiss liqueur chocolates. A bottle of top-hotel champagne and Swiss chocolates ought to have been expensive, but there was nothing else. We drank the champagne—it wasn't bad—and had only just finished the chocolates when two Russians sat down at the adjoining table.

Hearing English, they struck up a conversation. They both spoke impeccable English, and we enjoyed it so much that we ordered another bottle—again accompanied by Swiss liqueur chocolates.

After the second bottle, we decided to turn in and sleep off the effects. I went to the bar to ask for the bill, half expecting the worst—although Barnsley Council was paying. The waitress handed me a bill for thousands of roubles. I opened my wallet and showed her the sterling and US dollars.

She dug through the dollars, took a five-dollar bill, and handed me a bundle of roubles in change. Then, via the Russians, she explained she did not have enough money in the till to give me all my change—so if we returned the next day we had effectively prepaid for another bottle of champagne and chocolates. Marvellous what a five-dollar bill can buy.

The Ukrainians were in the process of building a restaurant to be called *Café Barnsley*. We saw it progress from visit to visit and, by the third trip, the shell was complete, with windows and external doors already installed. I often wondered what it was like once it opened.

Our three main hosts—Horlivka Yuri, Sergei and Eugene—made a return visit to Barnsley shortly before I left to join the Department of Trade and Industry.

The Export Adventurer

Back in South Yorkshire, I received a never-ending stream of referrals from the Chambers of Commerce and the Training and Enterprise Councils. At one point, I arranged a mini trade mission with the Rotterdam Chamber of Commerce. I took forty people to Holland, where one-to-one appointments had been arranged for all our delegates with potential trading partners.

The mission was a great success, even though, while we were in the Rotterdam Chamber building on 16 September 1992, we heard that sterling was in freefall—Black Wednesday—after John Major withdrew the pound from the ERM.

Our host's Chief Executive delivered a welcoming speech and included a few disparaging remarks about the state of the British economy. When it was my turn to respond, I pointed out that sterling had just fallen by 10%, meaning British exports were now 10% cheaper. As we were all exporters, the news was manna from heaven.

On another occasion, working with the Barnsley Business and Innovation Centre, we organised an "Interprise" inward trade mission which brought over 150 foreign businesses from Ireland, Denmark, Italy, France, Spain, Austria, Portugal, Germany, Luxembourg and Belgium to Barnsley and Doncaster.

We used the ballroom at Tankersley Manor in Barnsley and the Dome in Doncaster for one-to-one meetings with over two hundred local businesses. We ran a shuttle-bus service between the venues, and both Barnsley Council and Doncaster Council hosted dinners.

My time at Barnsley Chamber taught me how to operate between business-support organisations and local and central government.

The Export Adventurer

The DTI office in Leeds always sent a staff member to our export clubs and other events. They were genuinely impressed with what we were doing and started to promote the model to other Yorkshire chambers.

In 1993, one of the senior civil servants in Leeds introduced me to the Export Promoter concept and said I would be an ideal person to join the DTI. I read the programme and was immediately interested. The DTI were struggling to find someone to cover Korea. However, uprooting myself could have been detrimental to the Export Development Service.

By then, we had four staff in the export department. After discussion, we concluded that if we could find a replacement to run the service—and if I could have it written into my DTI contract that I would be available one day per month for the Chamber—then the service should cope.

In circumstances like that, the best option is to choose someone you know can do the job, and I knew exactly the person.

Patricia Bint had been in the Bartol export office when I left four years earlier and had since moved on to British Ropes in Doncaster. Patricia was a graduate member of the Institute of Export and very experienced. I contacted her and explained what the Export Development Adviser's role involved. Without needing much detail, she agreed to join Barnsley Chamber of Commerce as the replacement Export Development Adviser.

Chapter 34 — Department of Trade and Industry

In October 1993, I joined the Department of Trade and Industry. Although I was seconded rather than permanently appointed, I was subject to the same terms and conditions as any senior civil servant. I was required to sign a contract accepting those conditions, including being bound by the Official Secrets Act. Consequently, this chapter cannot be overly detailed.

Export Promoter — the role

In the early 1990s, the Government's integrated trade development work was delivered through the British Overseas Trade Board (BOTB), supported by local, regional, national and overseas operations. Its purpose was straightforward: to help British companies win business overseas.

Export Promoters were given a reasonably senior place within the hierarchy—something that mattered greatly in Government circles. I was frequently asked what "grade" I was, including by the Military Attaché. When I first arrived at the Embassy in Seoul, the First Secretary (Commercial) confirmed that, in formal terms, only the Ambassador and the Deputy Head of Mission outranked me. I largely ignored the status at the time, but I remember thinking it was not bad for a miner's son.

In practical terms, Export Promoters provided an essential link between the public and private sectors, and between UK companies and overseas investors, buyers and procurers.

The Export Adventurer

Most people involved would testify that the scheme worked. It generated business for UK companies both at home and overseas, strengthened relationships between Government and industry, and improved the UK's trading connections with international partners.

In the UK, Export Promoters worked closely with the country desks in the DTI. Overseas, we worked alongside the commercial sections in Embassies and High Commissions. Seeing the hard work pay off—when British companies won contracts—was genuinely gratifying. We could bring the right people together, at the right time, with the right objective.

The Export Promoter Initiative helped UK SMEs—and larger firms—win overseas business. It was the largest secondment programme from private industry in Whitehall. It gave companies something they rarely had access to: market and sector specialists with hands-on experience who could advise in plain English, introduce them to credible counterparts, and help open doors that were otherwise firmly shut.

My background in the Chamber of Commerce movement was an ideal bridge between the private sector and Government. Working inside Government gave me a unique insight into how the system operated and the depth of expertise available within the public sector. It also connected me with key contacts both in the UK and in Korea.

The Export Adventurer

A National Audit Office report later concluded that the Export Promoter Initiative was highly cost-effective, and that Export Promoters were the most effective service in securing the kinds of visits and contacts most likely to lead to orders. Better still, from the point of view of UK industry, the service was free.

I signed my civil service contract on 14 October 1993 for a fixed two-year period, commencing two weeks later. I was issued with a mobile phone, and a desk, filing cabinets, a laptop and printer, and my own letterheads were all delivered to me so that I could work from home. I was also provided with generous travel, subsistence and promotion budgets (first class on British Rail and business class in the air), and held the status and salary of a civil service Principal Officer.

One of my first trips was to Korea to meet the Ambassador, David Wright, and the entire commercial team. Embassies are staffed by British junior diplomats who progress from Third Secretary to Second and then First Secretary, but they are usually moved to another country every three years. Just as they become expert and genuinely useful, they move on. Fortunately, the local staff are permanent and know their own country and industries exceptionally well. They are the real experts.

The Export Adventurer

No two days were ever the same. One day you might be advising a major UK company on an acquisition or greenfield investment; the next, helping an SME manage a distributor relationship. The range was extraordinary: automotive components, fashion retailing, construction products, personal hygiene items—all in a single day. The challenge was aligning that breadth with what I knew about the market, but it meant learning new industries quickly and widening my contacts dramatically.

UK companies valued speaking to people who had "been there and done it". The support we offered ranged from individual company visits to seminars, clinics, conferences and pre-mission briefings; from leading trade missions to making introductions in-market and identifying genuine opportunities.

Working from Kingsgate House in London was impractical, so the DTI printed letterheads for me and I operated from home whenever I was not in Korea or visiting businesses across the UK.

Inward missions, seminars and Korea-focused work

We hosted an inward mission and trade conference from Korea comprising officials from the Korean Ministry of Trade

The Export Adventurer

and Industry and several notable captains of Korean industry, including the President of Hyundai Motors. On the British side, there were around twenty-five attendees, some with first-hand experience of Korea. These included Richard Needham, UK Minister for Trade and Industry; David Wright, who had just completed his posting as HM Ambassador to Korea; Sir Anthony Farrar-Hockley—GBE, KCB, DSO & Bar, MC—who had won his DSO following the Battle of the Imjin River at Hill 235 while serving with the "Glorious Gloucesters"; Max Hastings, whose book on the Korean War was published in 1987; and the Chair of the conference, Sir Howard Davies, then Director-General of the CBI. I was the sole DTI official present.

The mission and conference were held at the ICI Conference Centre in west London.

At another inward mission and seminar, held at the Carlton Towers Hotel and attended by ministers and senior officials from both countries, I gave a forty-minute presentation on the Korean market and trade opportunities. By then, it had become relatively straightforward. Armed with trade statistics and market demographics, I had built a comprehensive slide deck of around sixty slides covering everything required to promote Korea as a serious target market.

It was a wonderful two years. Before each visit to Korea, I would fax through a list of objectives. By the time I arrived, the Embassy's local commercial team had arranged the appointments. During this period, I visited major automotive plants, vast shipyards and electronics factories. As a British Government official, I was treated as a VIP almost everywhere I went.

I stood on giant shipyard cranes, lunched privately with the President of Hyundai Motors, and even travelled by helicopter from Pusan airport to the Samsung shipyard on Geoje Island. One Sunday, I joined an outing to Gloster Hill (as the Koreans spelled it), led by the British Military Attaché, who provided a running commentary on the battle. I climbed in and out of the actual foxholes used by the Glorious Gloucesters on Hill 235 during the famous Battle of the Imjin River.

Life working out of the Embassy was, frankly, a dream. The Ambassador had his driver and a Jaguar, and there were two additional Korean chauffeurs with large Korean cars for staff use. Availability was first come, first served, and sometimes the cars were tied up with commercial or consular duties. Even so, taxis were cheap and plentiful. Local travel was straightforward—provided you had time. Seoul congestion could turn a short journey into a slow procession.

I was not the only one who benefited from my secondment. Through seminars and presentations delivered across the UK—hosted by Chambers of Commerce, regional DTI offices, trade associations, and the Welsh, Scottish and Northern Ireland offices—many SMEs and larger firms began exporting to Korea or trading with Korean counterparts.

We also ran sector-specific seminars for the Department of Health and the Ministry of Defence. I built working relationships with the Small and Medium Industrial Promotion Corporation and the Korean Chamber of Commerce, which helped match British companies with appropriate counterparts in Korea.

Three transfers of technology took place during my two-year tenure, all originating from South Yorkshire.

The Export Adventurer

The 1994 UK trade mission to Korea

In 1994, Michael Heseltine led a "captains of industry" trade mission to Korea and Malaysia. Major British firms were represented, including Tarmac, Trafalgar House, Ove Arup, John Laing, Costain, Taylor Woodrow and Balfour Beatty.

At the time, British Airways operated services to Seoul via Hong Kong, originally introduced for the 1988 Seoul Olympics, but no airline flew directly from London to Seoul. Mr Heseltine, having recently survived a heart attack, required the ability to return to the UK within a single day if necessary. A non-stop flight was therefore essential.

There were nineteen of us on the aircraft. We assembled at the Royal Pavilion at Heathrow, with the aircraft parked alongside, and were treated to what could only be described as royal service—drinks and nibbles served before departure.

To make the non-stop 5,500-mile journey over Siberia, Mongolia and China possible using a 1990s-era Boeing 767, the aircraft underwent extensive modifications. It was stripped out to reduce weight and maximise fuel capacity. Most passenger seating was removed, with only the forward first- and business-class cabins retaining seats for the delegation.

Each of us was allocated three seats so that we could lie flat and sleep. The rear of the aircraft was left completely empty. I did peek through the curtain at one point and saw four men seated on folding chairs in the middle of the cavernous space—presumably the security team. With no conventional crew-rest facilities, British Airways cabin crew used inflatable beds laid out on the floor of the empty rear cabin during their rest periods.

The Export Adventurer

Because of the extraordinary flight length, the crew had to be doubled throughout: two pilots, two co-pilots, two flight engineers, and two complete cabin crews, with one team working while the other rested.

We were all issued sleeper suits and served meals, snacks and drinks whenever we asked. At the time, the Boeing 767 was regarded as a workhorse for mid- to long-range routes, but its fuel capacity and operational limits made a non-stop flight from the UK to East Asia a significant achievement.

What I did not realise then was that we were quietly making aviation history.

I had already worked alongside the Minister for Trade, Richard Needham MP, on several occasions at briefings and seminars, but until that day I had never met his boss, the Chairman of the Board of Trade.

I was taken forward and introduced to Mr Heseltine. He asked about my background and where I was from, but I kept the conversation firmly focused on trade—rather than on what was smouldering at the back of my mind at the time: mine closures.

On arrival in Seoul, the VIP treatment continued. We were escorted into a private reception lounge where Embassy commercial staff were waiting—one collecting passports, another baggage tags. While we refreshed ourselves, immigration clearance and baggage retrieval were handled entirely on our behalf.

Mr Heseltine was whisked away in the Ambassador's Jaguar to the Residence. The rest of us were taken to the super-deluxe Westin Chosun Hotel.

The following morning, at the British Embassy, I was introduced to Prince Edward, The Duke of Kent, in his capacity as Special Representative for International Trade and Investment. He lent his diplomatic influence and access to senior Korean officials and business leaders to facilitate high-level discussions.

The only other time I found myself on a flight with a government minister was entirely coincidental. I was travelling business class and was first in the queue to disembark at Tokyo Narita when Jeffrey Archer appeared beside me. He must have been the only passenger travelling first class.

At the jet bridge, a middle-aged Japanese official extended his hand in welcome. Jeffrey abruptly hung his briefcase on the man's fingers and said brusquely, "Carry that, will you?"

What it all gave me

My experience with the Department of Trade and Industry gave me a far deeper understanding of how the Korean Government—and inter-governmental relationships more broadly—actually operated, and how the interface between British Government, the Civil Service and business functioned in practice.

The Department also organised a four-day conference in Hong Kong for commercial staff from British Embassies and High Commissions, along with Export Promoters from across the Asia–Pacific region. Held at Government House and attended by around thirty participants, it provided an excellent opportunity to compare notes, exchange practical ideas, and understand what was—and was not—working across the region.

The Export Adventurer

With the handover of Hong Kong to China only a year or two away, those discussions were particularly timely.

Chapter 35 — North Korea

In 1994, I was approached by two businessmen who wanted to access North Korea but had no idea how to organise such a trip. After a few discussions with senior civil servants, it was agreed that it would be useful for me to go and take a look—on the proviso that it would be framed as a Barnsley Chamber of Commerce "mini-mission".

Setting it up took time because we needed visas, and at that point the UK had no diplomatic relations with North Korea. The nearest North Korean legation was in Paris. After some enquiries, it became clear that if we applied in person, the visas could be issued the same day. So the three of us arranged to meet at Waterloo Station and take the Eurotunnel train to Paris.

I left Doncaster in good time to reach King's Cross and get across London on the Tube to Waterloo. Unfortunately, GNER—the East Coast franchisee at the time—had a breakdown and I was delayed by an hour. By the time I reached King's Cross, it was already tight.

Despite my best efforts, I arrived on the platform at Waterloo three minutes after the train had departed. I'd kept my colleagues updated, so they knew where I was. I promptly turned around, went straight to London City Airport, and bought a ticket on the first flight to Charles de Gaulle.

Luck was on my side: there was a plane leaving in thirty minutes. I went straight through passport control and security into the departure lounge—and found it empty. I thought luck had deserted me again: the flight had boarded and gone without me.

The Export Adventurer

I was looking around the deserted lounge for someone to ask when a lady came through a door, walked directly up to me, and asked if I was the passenger for Air France to Paris. I confirmed, and she led me down some steps and out to a minibus. At the aircraft, I climbed the steps and boarded.

I was amazed. There was no one else on the flight.

It was a scheduled service, so if I hadn't turned up at the last minute, one assumes the aircraft would have departed empty. I was served breakfast and unlimited coffee and had my pick of newspapers. It was, for once, a very agreeable way to miss a train.

My time in the air was much less than my colleagues' time on the train because it was only in France that the TGV ran at full speed. In the UK—and through the tunnel—it trundled along at normal British pace. But Charles de Gaulle is a long way from central Paris, so the advantage didn't feel quite so dramatic by the time I got into the city.

I arrived at the North Korean trade legation about thirty-five minutes behind my colleagues. We were given coffee and then treated to an hour-long lecture on what we could and could not do—what we must and must not do—in North Korea.

One instruction stood out. On arrival in Pyongyang, we would be met by a guide who would take us first to the giant bronze statue of Kim Il Sung, who had died a year or so earlier. We were instructed that we must buy flowers and lay them at the feet of the "Great Leader".

They said they would arrange accommodation and took notes on the two businessmen's interests.

At that time the only ways into North Korea were via several regional Chinese airports, from Beijing International, or from Moscow. We had already planned to go via Beijing and had obtained our Chinese visas.

Pyongyang

On arrival in Pyongyang, we were met by two smart young men in sports jackets and trousers. They took us out to where two very large Japanese limousines were waiting. I and one escort got into the first car; my two colleagues and the other escort got into the second. We drove nose-to-tail through streets that were almost devoid of traffic.

The wide boulevards and building styles were not dissimilar to what was going up in South Korea—except everything in and around Pyongyang had the grey, utilitarian feel of a communist capital. Unlike Seoul, which was jam-packed with traffic, the only vehicles we saw were military trucks, a handful of cars, and the occasional trolleybus or tram.

The Export Adventurer

We were taken to an area that, in most cities, would have been an elite "stockbroker belt". In Pyongyang, it was a government visitor compound. We were shown to our rooms. The villa had the facilities of a five-star hotel—en-suite bathrooms and the like—and a large lounge, dining room, well-stocked library, kitchens, and perhaps eight or ten bedrooms in total.

After we'd freshened up, we were invited to the bar. It was astonishingly well stocked: at least fifteen Scotch whiskies, four or five brands of gin, and other spirits and wines from around the world.

Dinner was thoroughly Western, with four or five choices for each course. The food was well cooked and well presented.

After dinner, our hosts quizzed us again on what we hoped to achieve and then casually added a few items to the list of things they wanted us to look at—one of which was the prospect of finding a buyer for North Korean gold.

Our "minders", two guards, and the chef also stayed in the villa while we were there. One night I couldn't sleep and went down to the library at about 2 a.m., looking for English-language books. One of the minders appeared a few minutes later, fully dressed, and joined me in the library. That, in a single scene, told you everything you needed to know.

Five days under escort

We were there for five days. Each day we were driven everywhere in convoy, in the limousines. On the way, our hosts would often stop to show us tourist sites, including Kim Il Sung's birthplace near Pyongyang.

Almost all males between 18 and 45 were in military fatigues. Road repairs, construction sites, agricultural work—many of the people you saw were in uniform. Quite a lot of women in those age groups were also dressed in military clothing. So the claim that North Korea had one of the largest armies in East Asia was probably true in sheer headcount terms, although it did make you wonder how many were trained soldiers and how many were simply uniformed labour.

You also had to be careful what you said. Our hosts were heavily indoctrinated and genuinely believed they were technologically on equal terms with the West. They also believed South Koreans were effectively prisoners of the United States.

One evening they took us to the state circus. It was fantastic—every act absolutely perfect. Two identical twin acrobats were so precisely synchronised, movement for movement, that it was almost unnerving to watch. It was easily the most impressive circus performance I've ever seen.

They also took us to a department store in the large square often seen on television during the annual military parades. When we entered, the fluorescent lighting inside was flickering. As we progressed around the store, it became clear it was as much theatre as retail. The lights behind us were switched off; the lights ahead of us came on. When we changed floors, the escalator sprang to life just before we stepped on and died again as soon as we stepped off.

On the toy floor, the toys were metal pressings like the ones we had in the UK when I was a small boy. Drivers and passengers had faces painted onto the windows. There were no electric toys, only clockwork. It was like a museum exhibit—almost as if toy development had stopped in the 1950s.

On the streets we saw one or two new Mercedes 190s. The 190 was a new model in Europe then, so I asked why they were importing such an expensive car. I was told it wasn't imported—it was a 100% North Korean manufactured car. If Mercedes had anything similar, they must have copied it from them.

They took us to an industrial exhibition area and proudly showed us their "latest technology", including electro-erosion for manufacturing plastic injection mould tools. Having only recently left the pipe-and-fittings world, I knew perfectly well that this was not exactly cutting-edge outside North Korea—but after the Mercedes conversation, I thought it best to keep that to myself.

Leaving North Korea

On departure day, our hosts presented a bill for accommodation and food. It was extremely reasonable. We peeled off US dollar bills and settled it happily.

We flew out of Pyongyang to Beijing on a North Korean Air Koryo Russian-built aircraft. During taxiing, it threw out so much paraffin vapour that it seeped into the cabin and stung my eyes. I was very glad when we landed in Beijing and I could get a proper night's sleep at the Beijing Holiday Inn.

We couldn't remain in transit and fly straight on to Seoul because we couldn't check baggage from Pyongyang through to Seoul—for obvious security reasons. We had to clear our luggage in Beijing and check it in again for the onward flight, which forced an overnight stay.

At immigration in Seoul, the passport officer spotted the North Korean visa and became visibly excited. He asked what it was like and called over a couple of colleagues, who abandoned their booths for a few minutes. They had no objection at all to the fact that I'd been to North Korea; it was simply so rare for them to meet someone who had been that they wanted to know everything.

The following day, as soon as I arrived at the Embassy, I was asked to visit the Military Attaché—who also wanted to hear, in detail, exactly what I had seen.

Chapter 36 — Korea Connections

When my secondment to the Department of Trade and Industry ended in October 1995, it was clear to me that there was insufficient practical support for most UK small and medium-sized enterprises seeking to access non-traditional—but highly valuable—markets such as South Korea.

The DTI's overseas trade services could provide lists of potential contacts, but very few SMEs had either the experience or the financial resilience to pursue anything other than the most obviously promising leads. Korea, in particular, demanded time, persistence, cultural understanding, and repeated visits—resources that most SMEs simply did not have.

Formation of Korea Connections

Korea Connections was established by my Korean wife, Dominique (Cho Hye Young), and me at the conclusion of my two-year secondment to the DTI in 1995.

By that point, I could reasonably claim the following background:

- One of Michael Heseltine's original one hundred senior businesspeople seconded to the DTI in 1993 as Export Promoters
- Ten years of Korean trading experience
- Regular contact with over two hundred Korean businesses
- Four years living and working in Korea
- Married to a Korean national since 1989

- First technology transfer to Korea in 1985
- Spending alternate months living in Korea and the UK during the mid-1980s

This experience, combined with an extensive network in both the private and public sectors in Korea and the UK, placed us in a unique position to assist British companies in accessing the Korean market effectively.

Overview

Korea became a member of the OECD in 1996, marking its formal arrival among the world's developed economies. Yet despite being the world's eleventh-largest economy, it ranked only as the twenty-fifth largest export destination for British goods.

In short, the UK was not getting its fair share.

Over the previous decade, I had built strong relationships across Korean industry, government, and trade bodies. Through my secondment, I had also developed deep connections within the UK public sector. Korea Connections was designed to bring these networks together for the benefit of British industry.

Cultural Requirements

Korean and Western business cultures differ in many fundamental ways. Getting these wrong can end a business relationship before it even begins; getting them right is an absolute prerequisite.

Unlike Southeast Asian nations, Korea has never been a Western colony. As a result, business is conducted in a distinctly Korean—and more broadly East Asian—way. Personal relationships must be established, nurtured, and maintained before any meaningful business can take place.

British SMEs rarely had the resources to visit Korea often enough to build these relationships. Korea Connections filled that gap. Several companies used our Seoul office as their local liaison office, enabling them to demonstrate a genuine and continuous commitment to the market.

Some clients used our services to enter Korea for the first time. Some operated directly, though most appointed agents or distributors identified through our research. Others sought licensees or required assistance resolving existing problems.

We offered a fully tailored range of services covering every stage of market entry: assessment, establishment, growth, and long-term maintenance.

Dominique Bratley (Cho Hye Young)

My wife, Dominique, became one of the UK's most highly recognised professional Korean interpreters and translators. She was frequently called upon to provide simultaneous interpretation in European courts and at hearings in London, Geneva, and Amsterdam.

A Korean national with exceptional English-language skills, she followed her father—who had been a translator for the American Army—into language services. Her education spanned Korea, New England, and Los Angeles. She graduated from Sheffield University with a BA (Honours) in

Business Studies and had worked for large publicly listed companies in Korea, the United States, and the UK.

Services Offered

From our UK office, we provided:

- Market assessment and product suitability analysis
- Advice on correct cultural approach
- Full translation, interpretation, and printing services
- Cross-cultural awareness briefings

Our Korean office was permanently staffed by bilingual personnel who supported business development on the ground. Services included:

- Identifying competitors and their agents
- Identifying and short-listing potential agents or distributors
- Arranging full itineraries and confirmed appointments for visiting clients
- Providing representation and liaison office services when clients were not in Korea
- Managing and motivating agents, distributors, licensees, and joint ventures
- Keeping clients informed of new developments, tenders, and projects

Globalisation and Opportunity

At the time, "globalisation" was the prevailing buzzword. The Korean government had recognised the necessity of full engagement in international trade. Korea was a signatory to all major conventions on intellectual property, free trade, and environmental protection, and had joined both the OECD and the WTO.

Major Korean chaebol—Samsung, Daewoo, LG, Hyundai, and Halla—had invested heavily in manufacturing operations in the UK. British industry clearly needed to build relationships with these companies, but such engagement often required initial contact and credibility to be established in Korea itself.

Korea Connections provided that bridge, particularly for SMEs.

Case Studies and Successes

We undertook a market study for one of the UK's largest importers of automotive aftermarket parts. This resulted in container-load consignments of Korean-manufactured car batteries, brake pads, and filters being supplied to the UK market.

For a major high-street discount retailer, we researched the Korean ceramics market for crockery, leading to many years of sustained trade.

Working with the Korean Small and Medium Industrial Promotion Corporation, we matched British technology providers with Korean partners in high-tech mixing plants and fibre-optic lighting.

We were the first organisation to introduce Korean-made reversing sonar to the UK. Initially supplied to local authorities for refuse collection vehicles, this expanded into sonar integrated with CCTV. Today, such systems are standard on buses, coaches, and refuse vehicles.

The Export Adventurer

We represented a Peterborough-based manufacturer of heavy-plant seating. Almost every piece of plant produced by Hyundai Heavy Industries in Ulsan was fitted with one of their seats.

We supported the UK's leading wind tunnel manufacturer. While the wind tunnel itself was not sold, high-value measuring components were successfully supplied for existing installations.

Nearly every Daewoo truck and bus incorporated British-made silicone turbo hoses. These were designed in Crawley and shipped to Korea. I visited Daewoo's R&D facility near Anyang more than thirty times.

We assisted a UK company supplying components to Korea's extensive power station construction programme, which at one point exceeded one hundred new plants.

Another client developed technology to melt basalt rock into fibres for silencer insulation. With a higher melting point than glass fibre, basalt proved ideal for Korean automotive applications.

We also represented a British company that developed a water-vapour combustion enhancement system for petrol and diesel engines. Daewoo provided a vehicle for R&D, recognising the technology's potential for cleaner, more efficient combustion.

Our work spanned a wide range of products: metal-removal tools, enzymes, paint technology, hose clamps, toys, quality-control equipment, boilers, garments, plumbing fittings, pumps, and more.

Closing Reflections

Working with such a diverse portfolio was both challenging and immensely rewarding. We enjoyed significant successes and experienced the occasional disappointment. As I have always believed, the harder you work, the luckier you become.

Chapter 37 — Retirement

The Export Development Service

I returned to, and continued with, the Export Development Service until my retirement in 2021. During that time, I helped establish and support a number of businesses, acting as a director in the start-up phase of the following companies:

- Tabard International Ltd
- Telewatch Ltd
- Motorsonics Ltd
- International Trade Facilities Ltd
- UK Import Corporation Ltd

I gave my time to the Export Development Service on a free-of-charge basis, claiming only the reimbursement of expenses. After a lifetime spent in international trade, it felt right to give something back.

The enjoyment, friendships, travel, and income that international trade provided over the years were more than I could ever have expected. Few careers offer such a combination of intellectual challenge, cultural exposure, and human connection.

I wholeheartedly recommend international trade as a vocation. It rewards curiosity, resilience, adaptability, and integrity—and it repays effort many times over.

Conclusion

I could not have asked for a more interesting or more exhilarating working life. What I gained along the way more than compensated for the countless hours spent alone—in smart hotels, airport lounges, and at 35,000 feet. There was a price, of course. In my case, it was the loss of a conventional family life. But the trade-off was a life lived at full stretch.

Looking back, many of my most successful contracts can be traced to a single decision: George Bell's determination to exhibit at the Baghdad Fair in 1981. That choice led me to discover that several chaebol-owned Korean contractors were already active in Iraq on major projects. Follow-up visits to Korea and India prompted my recommendation to exhibit at the World Trade Centre in Seoul, which in turn led to Mr Kang's interest—and ultimately to licensed manufacturing in Korea.

Once we had successfully established a factory under licence, we gained not only production capability but confidence. That confidence bred momentum, and momentum opened doors elsewhere. I identified New Zealand as a priority market because of its widespread use of high-temperature, geothermally heated water—and because Dave Picton was already extruding polybutylene there. He was not interested, but Mico Wakefield were.

If there is a lesson in all of this, it is that sales are not driven by spreadsheets alone. Research and planning matter, but so does instinct—the ability to sense opportunity, join the dots, and act before the moment passes.

Since I entered international trade in the late 1960s, the world—and the way business is conducted—has changed beyond recognition.

The Export Adventurer

Nowhere has that transformation been more dramatic than in communications.

In the early years, international communication was dominated by telegrams and cables, where messages were charged by the word. Brevity was not a stylistic preference but a financial necessity. Every extra word quite literally cost money. That constraint shaped how people wrote and thought, giving rise to a compressed working language of abbreviations and acronyms.

A message such as *"MUM SPARES ETA 16th STOP"* translated into *"Most Urgent Message: spares estimated time of arrival 16th."* Meaning was packed into the fewest possible words, and punctuation itself carried a price.

The telex system that followed—essentially two typewriters connected through the telephone network—was more flexible, but it inherited the same habits. Messages were still written with economy and precision, because time, cost, and clarity all mattered.

The arrival of the fax machine in the early 1980s felt revolutionary. For the first time, documents could be transmitted across the world in minutes rather than days. Then came email—slow, unreliable, and cumbersome at first, but utterly transformative. Today, drawings, contracts, photographs and data can be created and transmitted instantly from a phone or laptop to anywhere on the planet.

At the start of my career, finding a manufacturer meant poring over heavy reference books such as *Kelly's Merchants and Manufacturers Directory*. Today, the global marketplace sits on a screen. Markets, competitors, suppliers and customers are all just a few keystrokes away.

Historically, business demanded face-to-face contact. To understand a market, build trust, or close a deal, someone had to get on a plane. With hindsight, at least ninety per cent of my travel could have been replaced by video conferencing had today's technology existed. The world now resides in your home or office.

What once required time, stamina, expense and perseverance is now limited largely by imagination and initiative. The tools have changed, but the fundamentals have not. Relationships still matter. Trust still has to be earned. Cultural understanding remains critical.

Ironically, despite all this technological progress, communication itself has arguably declined. We are deluged with emails, important messages drown in noise, calls go unanswered, and automated systems replace people. One individual with a computer now does the work once shared among many with calculators and typewriters. Flight times may be shorter, but modern airports and security have become hostile environments in their own right.

And yet—despite all of that—I would choose the same path again without hesitation.

International trade gave me challenge, purpose, friendships, curiosity, and a front-row seat to a changing world. It demanded resilience and adaptability, but it repaid effort many times over. Few careers offer such breadth of experience, such cultural richness, or such a sense of having genuinely lived.

If you have the appetite for uncertainty, the patience to learn, and the courage to step beyond the familiar, international trade remains one of the most rewarding vocations imaginable.

The Export Adventurer

Appendices

Appendix I – Airlines Used

Aer Lingus
Aeroflot
Air Canada
Air China
Air France
Air India
Air Ivoire
Air Koryo
Air Malta
Air New Zealand
Air UK
Alitalia
All Nippon Airways
American Airlines
Ansett
Antonov Airlines
Asiana Airlines
Australian Airlines
Austrian Airlines
BMI Regional
British Airways
British Caledonian

The Export Adventurer

British Eagle
British Midland
BWIA (British West Indies Airways)
Cathay Pacific
China Airlines
China Flying Dragon Aviation
Continental Airlines
Cyprus Airways
Delta Air Lines
EgyptAir
Emirates Airline
Etihad Airways
Finnair
Garuda Indonesia
Gulf Air
Iberia
Iraqi Airways
Japan Airlines
Jet2
Jetstar
KLM Cityhopper
KLM Royal Dutch Airlines
Korean Air
Kuwait Airways
LIAT (Leeward Islands Air Transport)
Lufthansa
Malaysia Airlines
Middle East Airlines
Midwest Airlines
Monarch Airlines
Northwest Orient Airlines
Olympic Air
Pan American World Airways (Pan Am)
Philippine Airlines
Qantas
Royal Jordanian

The Export Adventurer

Ryanair
Sabena
Scandinavian Airlines
Singapore Airlines
Sri Lankan Airlines
Swissair
TAP Air Portugal
Thai Airways International
Thomas Cook Airlines
Thomson Airways
Tigerair Australia
Trans Australian Airways
Turkish Airlines
Trans World Airlines (TWA)
United Airlines
Vancouver Island Air
Virgin Atlantic Airways
Virgin Blue Australia
Windward Islands Airways
Winlink (Windward Islands)
XL Airways

Appendix II – Countries Visited on Business
(add 20 more where I have vacated)

Country	Number of Visits
Andorra	1
Abu Dhabi	2
Antigua & Barbuda	4
Australia	16
Austria	4
Bahrain	8
Barbados	4
Belgium	13
Bosnia and Herzegovina	1
Brunei Darussalam	1
Canada	1
China	3
Côte d'Ivoire	1
Croatia	3
Cyprus	1
Denmark	6
Dubai	6
Egypt	1
Finland	3
France	23
The Gambia	1
Germany	17
Ghana	1
Greece	3
Hong Kong	64
India	2

The Export Adventurer

Country	Number of Visits
Iraq	14
Ireland	6
Italy	9
Japan	5
Jordan	16
Korea (North)	1
Korea (South)	60
Kuwait	1
Lebanon	1
Liberia	1
Liechtenstein	1
Luxembourg	4
Macedonia	1
Malaysia	55
Malta	1
Montenegro	2
New Zealand	3
Nigeria	1
Northern Ireland	4
Palestinian State*	1
Papua New Guinea	1
Philippines	1
Portugal	1
Sierra Leone	1
Spain	15
Sri Lanka	12
St Kitts & Nevis	1
St Lucia	4

The Export Adventurer

Country	Number of Visits
St Vincent	4
Sweden	5
Switzerland	11
Togo	1
The Netherlands	25
Trinidad/Tobago	4
Thailand	1
Tunisia	1
Turkey	2
Ukraine	3
United States	13

* As recognised at the time of visit.

Appendix III – Aircraft Types Flown

Airbus A300 – medium-range wide-body
Airbus A310
Airbus A320
Airbus A321 – narrow-body
Airbus A330
Airbus A340
Airbus A350

BAC One-Eleven – jet airliner

Boeing 707 – medium/long-range
Boeing 727 – short/medium-range narrow-body
Boeing 737 – short/medium-range narrow-body
Boeing 747 – long-range high-capacity wide-body
Boeing 757 – medium/long-range narrow-body
Boeing 767 – medium/long-range wide-body
Boeing 767 – Modified for extra-long journey
Boeing 777 – long/ultra-long-range wide-body

Bristol 175 Britannia – long-range turboprop

Britten-Norman Islander – commuter
Britten-Norman Trislander – commuter

de Havilland Canada DHC-3 Otter

Douglas DC-9 – jet
Douglas DC-10 – wide-body trijet

Fokker F27 / Fairchild F27 – turboprop
Fokker F28 – regional jet
Fokker 50 – turboprop regional

The Export Adventurer

Fokker 70 – regional jet
Fokker 100 – regional jet

Ilyushin Il-96

Lockheed L-1011 TriStar – wide-body trijet

McDonnell Douglas MD-11 – long-range trijet
McDonnell Douglas MD-81/82/83/88 – short/medium-range
McDonnell Douglas MD-87 – medium-range
McDonnell Douglas MD-90 – medium-range

Shorts 330 – regional airliner

Tupolev Tu-154 – medium-range

www.ingramcontent.com/pod-product-compliance
Lightning Source LLC
Chambersburg PA
CBHW020632220526
45464CB00001B/111